BIG BROTHER, BIGFOOT

CONNOR FLYNN

BEYOND THE FRAY
Publishing

ISBN 13: 978-1-954528-34-5

Cover design: Disgruntled Dystopian Publications

Beyond The Fray Publishing, a division of Beyond The Fray, LLC, San
Diego, CA
www.beyondthefraypublishing.com

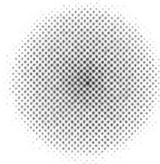

BEYOND THE FRAY

Publishing

CONTENTS

CHAPTER 1
INITIATION

Searching for the Caveman

The missing link between man and our creator may be closer than we could ever imagine. According to reports from all over the world, dating back to the beginning of time, man has never been alone. My name is Connor the Countryman, and I believe our connection in the forest can provide us the answers to the questions of the skies. There is a pyramid on our dollar, and a giant on the 2000 New Hampshire quarter. The truth's tide stays determined by leaking through. People have been vanishing from national parks and other dense areas by the hundreds, so when adventuring out in the wilderness, please take caution! And beware of the one born feet first with eyebrows that meet!

Signs of Sasquatch come in many forms. Chances are, we all have walked right past a Bigfoot structure while out hiking in the woods. Tree knocks, rock smacks, and ground stomps are just a few ways the creatures communicate through the environment. They verbalize using whoops, hoots, groans, growls, and moans. They have their own language that consists of ingenious words and tongue clicks often referred to as samurai chatter. Their vocal range exceeds the limits of any human being. If you happen to stumble across arches, tree breaks, rock stacks, balanced logs, and tipi structures, there is a good chance that the wildman is near. Check the dirt for long lines, perfect circles, and other ground glyphs.

These humanoid creatures are mentioned in the Bible, Quran, and many ancient texts. In the Indian *Ramayana* from 400–700 BC, there is mention of an advanced race of monkey species named Vanara. Vana meaning forest and Nara meaning man. The prophecy states they shared hot purified water called Shilajit with humans. The magical liquid helped the humans develop physically, mentally and, most importantly, spiritually. The tincture is good for the pineal gland and directly hydrates the soul. There are many statues and temples in India of these deities, and they are still worshipped to this day.

Me and Mireya Mayor at the Great Bigfoot Conference discussing dolphins and Bigfoot.

In the Bible, Esau is an Edomite and is covered in a thick coat of reddish brown hair. He preferred sleeping outside and hunting venison. Cain is the son of Adam and Eve and was also known as the marked one. But most interesting is the Nephilim from the Book of Enoch. The sons of God came to Earth and impregnated the daughters of Earth, creating titans, demigods, and fallen ones. The watchers watched and waited for a window of opportunity. We forgot them, and they have snuck back into our sanctuary.

The good book describes the era of days when giants roamed the surface, dragons soared the skies, and leviathans patrolled the deep blue seas. The fallen angels were determined to spread evil through the world, but God emptied the heavens, and it rained down from the firmament, flooding our realm, turning the behemoths to stone. Mud fossils surround us today. Take a second look at that mountain; it used to be alive.

People know me as the Bigfoot guy. I grew up fishing, hunting and urban exploring. I was obsessed with horror movies and unsolved mysteries. I chase waterfalls and cryptids. I bike, kayak, and rock climb where I can. I was in the geology society and the outdoor adventure club in high school. I wrote for the school newspaper and did a lot of freelance. I played quidditch and made films at Bowling Green. I stage-managed a punk rock musical and umpired/refereed sports. But my main passion is expanding my knowledge on mysteries and cryptids across the planet.

I lived out of my car across the United States and met many interesting people. I slept under bridges and at marinas, twenty-four-hour grocery stores, and dead-end roads. While couchsurfing, you meet the people you need. When you follow your destined path, all your needs are met in abundance. Hobo is short for home-body. I was a hobo, and I still am. Hitting rock bottom isn't always a bad thing. The darkest nights are usually followed by the brightest days.

Through bigfootanonymous, I have narrated over five hundred Sasquatch encounters and interviewed countless people about their cryptid experience. I have spoken to people who have fed Harry, been touched by the creature, and others who camped at Bluff Creek. We have covered troglodytes, fairies, Indian mounds, werewolves, spelunking, war stories, police cases and of course gnat man. But my best stories were off the record... until now. This is a collection of experiences, journals, and encounters that I have been putting together since before the millennium.

I was covering fire-breathing dragons in the fourth grade, the same year United 93 flew right over my school. But articles of wildman encounters and giant bone excavations go back to the beginning of news and press. The hunt for the German wild man, the Lovelock Giants, and of course David versus Goliath. Native tribes all around the planet have stories and lore that surround these beings. The yeren, the yeti, and the yowie are being spotted to this day. I have been in the same building as Yao Ming, Shawn Bradley and Shaquille O'Neal. They all have the giant gene, and their presence is felt when you are nearby.

There is an old Irish tale about a farmer named Connor who lost his two cows. He searched for them all day, and he found shelter in the night. The door was answered by a tall old woman, and they were expecting him. Three men surrounded him and transformed into wolves. They surrounded him and licked their chops. Connor started swinging his walking stick erratically, and the eldest wolf yelled at him to stop. The elder made the crazies disperse.

The wolf asked if he remembered a young wolf with a thorn through his side. Connor remembered. He had nursed it back to health. That pup was the eldest wolf. He offered him a safe place for the night and promised he would not be bothered. He woke up the next morning on a hay bale in his own yard. He was confused, but that was the best sleep he had ever gotten.

His cows were still gone, but three new ones were in his pasture. The eldest wolf was there and herded them. They grew to be the greatest cows in the land while Connor became rich and successful. My homeland's proverb goes "Lessons are won by a good deed done." All beasts aren't monsters.

There is artwork of religious figures with wolves, hieroglyphs of men the size of giraffes and elephants the size of pyramids! Where did those giants run off to? There are plenty of tales of vampires and wildmen in my homeland. The fountain of youth is real, and the sun is much smaller than they say. Heaven is a real physical place but so is hell.

The military, national park service, and police have encounters dating back to opening day. Pilots, truckers, and loggers are well aware of their existence. There have been blood, hair, urine, fecal, and saliva samples. The hair follicles have transparent characteristics. This allows the creatures to camouflage themselves with their surroundings. Many tracks have unique dermal ridges. Their skeleton is very flexible, similar to a bug. They are double jointed and sometimes crawl like spiders. They are true apex predators. They sense UV rays and can sense meditation, psychedelics, and even disability. Check out Trollhunter for an inside look!

Troglodytes can mimic animals, machines, and even loved ones with their powerful diaphragm and vocal cords. The Sierra Sounds and Ohio Howls both have voice waves that human vocal capacities can't physically reach. These creatures aren't humans that have become primitive, they are the true ancient species of man. The true natives of Earth. The Sumerian Tablets may be more accurate than recently accredited.

Infrasound, sonar locating, and telepathic senses are natural to their brain and abilities. If humans' air, water, and food were not poisoned, I truly believe we would have some degree of their sixth sense. These apex predators take advantage of night vision and occupy the endless subterranean chambers of Earth. They thrive near mountains and volcanoes but could be anywhere that deer and rabbit live.

The existence of Sasquatch is still widely debated today. Even though there is a mountain of evidence and a list of witnesses that could stretch from pole to pole, the elusive beast is still an unsolved mystery to mainstream media and science. The obvious cover-up just fuels the fire more. There is a divine energy around these creatures, and I believe they are our closest bridge to our creator, so let's cross it! People deserve to know what's out there so we can properly protect our families. There is a chance we can learn from them and maybe achieve peace in future generations. Look at the story of the Grinch.

The quest for Sasquatch is very close to my heart and soul. The abominable snowman and Harry were a big part of my childhood. My family members have had encounters, and others refused to even discuss the topic. I always liked to dig where I wasn't supposed to. The creature's existence is obvious. I'm more interested to see if they are angels or demons. Let's cross that bridge when there are no cars. This journey started targeting bigfoot but has led me down a path of werewolves, swamp things, and many other beings that walk this Earth among us.

CHAPTER 2
OHIO GRASSMAN
THE HEART OF IT ALL

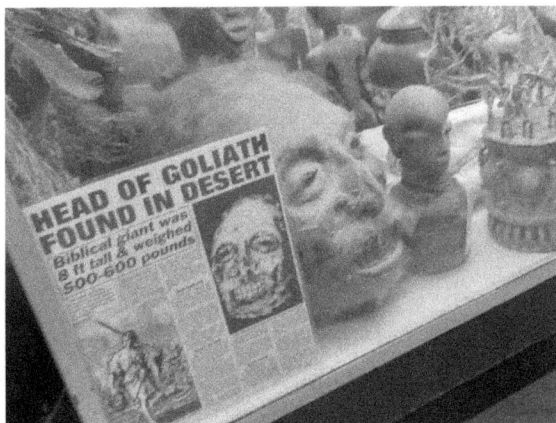

Am I David? Head of Goliath from Marie
Laveau's Voodoo Museum

The Buckeye State is famous for astronauts, *Nightmare on Elm Street*, and the creation of Superman, but the Ohio grassman would even scare Jeffrey Dahmer out of the woods. With sightings going back to the days of the Mohican, the Buckeye Beast has let his reign be known through the Ohio Valley. A renegade species of wildman, the grassmen are far more aggressive than the typical evasive Sasquatch. The legend began when two giant chiefs came to a disagreement over war with the humans and the abduction of their women and children.

There are more than ten thousand burial mounds in the state of Ohio. Giants have been discovered in Toledo, Chillicothe, and across the river from Wheeling and Moundsville. The natives who called the Buckeye State home have legends and lore warning of dangerous cannibalistic timber giants. The Indians traded with peaceful mound builders and went to war with the more aggressive clans. The Cleveland Browns are dogmen, not dawgs.

These tribes mark their territory with many different scents and structures. They urinate and spray around the perimeter to keep humans and other Sasquatch away. They will bend trees, lay nests and build teepee structures. They will create these shelters with fallen limbs and logs but sometimes use entire trees. Giant fifty-foot wickiups have been discovered. Usually the trees are stripped of bark and broken off at the base. Five or six broken trees will be placed against a central strong standing tree, and that will be the primary part of the camp.

In August 1972, three different people were attacked by a beast in a small northwest town. Witnesses claimed they saw an eight-foot monster with hairy feet. Some claimed it was an aggressive grassman, but the town remembers it as the Werewolf of Defiance. The creature was spotted running like a caveman carrying a giant stick. The entire town was on high alert and is still on edge to this very day.

One night, we snuck out of my friend's house to pull some pranks and meet up with some girls. We ding-dong ditched a couple of houses and lit off firecrackers in the sewer tunnels. The police were patrolling, and we ran into the park in the corner of the neighborhood. The cops pulled in, so we went deep into the woods and got separated.

I was terrified of getting caught, so I was blinded by adrenaline. I kept moving at a good pace and ran into the creek. I knew I would be able to navigate the area using that. I crept silently in the water, using the small rapids to mask my sound, when I heard a rustling up in the leaves ahead of me. I crept out onto the bank and quietly tried to call out to one of my friends. I was met by a deafening silence, so I approached the tree that I heard the noise from.

I took one step forward and was met with a rumbling below my feet. It sent a jolt up my knee and paralyzed me in a compromised stance. I teared up instantly and knew I had overstepped my boundary. I tried to open my hands as I backed into the creek. I ditched my lighter at the edge of the treeline, to hide the evidence and to thank the monster for just issuing me a warning.

One of my friends is from that same neighborhood. He is a security guard, ayahuasca shaman, and film-maker. He says he encountered a brown shadow creature about ten feet tall in the same woods. He also told me that he sometimes turns into a wolf while meditating and has the fur to prove it. I'm not sure if I encountered my buddy along the creek or his arch-nemesis.

That was not the only time we encountered something strange in Medina County. Near Sleepy Hollow, there were stories of a creature that lurked through the woods in my friend's region. Alex called him the wolf-man, but his dad simply called it "the Beast". He warned us that the creature could smell fear and that we should stay inside after dark. Part of me just thought it was a ploy to stop us from sneaking out, but I would soon realize that he was being dead serious.

We had our golf league the next morning, so there were no plans of mischief. We spent the night in Alex's basement and watched *Saving Private Ryan*. He had a walk-out patio that led directly into the woods. There was a creek, and it was the perfect den for a predator. We made little jokes throughout the night and moved quickly when we grabbed snacks, but it was just an ordinary sleepover.

Right before bed, everything changed. We were shooting pool, and an eerie feeling swept over the floor. Collectively, we all caught onto the strange vibe and began investigating. We crawled out of direct view and began peering through the smaller windows. That was when we spotted some glowing eyes. They were about six feet off the ground and meant to intimidate. We received the message and knew we were being stalked. The wolfman was real. The wolfman was close.

Face at Worden's Ledges.

We were paralyzed in fear. After what felt like hours, we crawled back behind the couch, shivering with chills. We tried to go to sleep, but that was impossible. We kept peeking back toward the woods to see if we could get a visual, but it was to no avail. After an hour of stone-cold panic, we booked it upstairs and slept in his room. The next morning it all felt like a dream, but we knew what we'd seen. The wolfman was born; the dogman was near.

Not long after, Jake and Alex had another encounter with this mysterious beast. They were getting a ride home from the rec center with a fireman one evening. They turned into his development, and they spotted a wolf creature cross the road on two legs. The beast scaled a steep cliffside and ran off toward a barn. I had the boys write incident reports independently, and both their stories matched. There is definitely a large cryptid patrolling the woods of Sleepy Hollow.

My grandparents own a 180-acre farm in south-eastern Ohio near Wheeling and Moundsville, West Virginia. There have been many bigfoot sightings in the Ohio Valley, but the ancient burial mounds are what's most interesting. There have been hundreds of skeletons excavated that are proof that giants existed in the Americas.

Recently my mom's cousin Eddie told me a story about an encounter he had while hunting on the property. Before the sun rose, he was heading out to his tree stand and was being followed by something walking bipedal. When he would stop, it would stop. He said a feeling of dread overtook every other emotion inside him. Ed changed his route and wrote it off as his mind playing tricks on him.

When I was younger, I was hiking near the same location with my good friend Jake. We were accompanied by my black Lab Seico and my grandparents' two blue heelers, Shep and Joey. After miles of adventure, we stopped below the grandchildren's tree house for a breather. After a couple of minutes, we heard a strange noise above us, and a black creature dropped... right on top of us!!

It all happened so fast. But Jake and I took off running. The dogs were squealing and barking at this thing. They surrounded it. At first glance, I thought it was a bear or panther. For years I told myself it was a giant feral cat. Recently Jake said, "That thing was as big as Seico!"

We made it to the yard and started worrying about the dogs. We could still hear the strange noises from down in the valley. But after a couple of minutes, they finally came running up. They had a look on their faces and were acting strange the rest of the night. My grandpa has found large unidentifiable scat on the property and has had to shoot the gun to save the cattle on multiple occasions. There were escaped ostriches nearby and many bobcats. Now I think it may have been a juvenile dogman.

A decade later, we were camping in my backyard for a blood moon eclipse. Around 2 a.m., we were lying in the grass, enjoying the sky's show, when we heard some shuffling on the other side of my barn. At first we thought it was my cats chasing prey but then realized that they were lying nearby. We figured it was a deer and went back to the stars.

After a few minutes, we could feel a rumbling in our

chests. There was a strong reverb from a low growl on the other side of the barn. That was no deer. The cats were spooked too. We got up to investigate but could barely see and only had a stick for protection. We chose to lay back down and accept our fate. We internally surrendered, but the weird feeling went away after a while, and we were back to the skies.

The woods across the street have many strange occurrences. There are witch stones, abandoned cabins, and homeless hangouts. Strange lights and glowing orbs were nothing new. A picture of the Whitney Monster looks exactly like the transparent crawler creature crossing the road that I saw one misty night. I'm not sure if the creature that approached us on the blood moon eclipse looked more like Gollum or Azog, but it sure spooked us. I think it just sensed our psychedelic vibrations and wanted to check us out.

CHAPTER 3
YOUGHIOGHENY YOWIE
OHIOPYLE STATE PARK

Sketch of the Yowie

The Youghiogheny has been a crucial footpath through the mountains for animals, gatherers, and even our first president, George Washington. The river is famous for its rainbow trout fishing and white water rafting. The waters also played a major role in the French and Indian War and the expansion of mining across Pennsylvania. In the core of the Laurel Highlands, the Yough is usually remembered for good days and unique adventures, but the surrounding soil holds a history of more complicated times. With stories of hostile Sasquatch harassing hunters and an old Indian tale of an aquatic beast named Ogua, these depths hold more mysteries than just Dimple Rock.

Fayette County is no stranger to bigfoot sightings. Newspapers and magazines covered multiple encounters in the '70s. Kids were chased out of the woods by red eyes, and the entire region went crazy. Footprints, twisted trees, and animal skeletons have been found in different parts of the county. There have been loud screams that sound like dying women that rain from the valley.

Creatures have been spotted watching four-wheelers, eating apples in the orchard and terrorizing campers. In 2001, a couple was lapping their tent by a Sasquatch intimidating them by screaming and grunting throughout the night. One hiker watched the creature add a protective layer of sticks to an outcropping of rock. Another duo encountered a bush shaking like a windstorm before being chased off by the beast. Sadly, there have been many disappearances in the nearby area.

In an unnamed nearby remote neighborhood, everyone on the six-mile road has had their own encounters with the "Old Man". He has spooked hunters, stolen fishermen's trout, and is heard knocking and screaming through the day and night. The locals have fed him carrots, old refrigerator food, and watermelon. Although, he didn't know how to eat it until the woman broke it open; then it was all gone by the next morning. When the summer ended and the melons were no longer for sale, he let his anger be known. He has left flowers on the back steps of the woman and follows her while hiking. The grandmother can sense how the Sasquatch is feeling and that he is telepathic with her, but she still doesn't trust him. There have been lights in the sky and lights in the same woods, so she doesn't know if he is an alien or just an old man.

I was the youngest out of six guys, and it was going to be my first time on white water. They told me that there had been some casualties on the river, so I was already feeling nervous. We were staying at the Summit Inn, famous for the view and infamous for the legends. Down the trail from the Laurel Highlands, this area was rich in history and mystery. It was my dad, two other firemen, their sons, and a middle school me.

The first night we explored the grounds, swam in the pool, and told stories at a local pub. That was cut short when we were horsing around and the older guys were roughing me up. I barricaded myself in the bar's phone booth and pretended to call the cops. It actually dialed, and I hung up when it started ringing. Then they called back. Mazz picked up the phone and said, "They just left!" while escorting us back to the hotel.

We sat outside drinking beers as the sun went down.

We admired the scenic view and were engulfed in excitement for the morning adventure. We heard howls in the distance, and it reminded me of my grandparents' farm. Flashbacks of hiking the holler and tracking deer rushed back to me. I felt like it was the night before the hunt. I was ready for the adrenaline.

On the way back to the room, I definitely understood why many visitors think the Summit is haunted. The vintage pictures seem to follow you down the hall and tuck you in goodnight. It's a true all-inclusive resort. I fell asleep within minutes of meeting the pillow. I was treated to dreams of Tarzan adventures and insane car chases. I felt like a tackle dummy when I woke up, but breakfast got me right back to where I needed to be.

We drove to the river, and my eyes lit up when I saw hundreds of people carrying rafts and kayaks. Goosebumps filled my arms, and I knew I was exactly where I needed to be. We checked in and waited for the safety course meeting. We listened to the experts and took mental notes. Do not try to stand up in the river. Point your toes up and reach for the rope. "Hold on tight" was all I needed to hear.

We had decades of experience in the raft, so we vowed not to use one of their guides. I hesitated at first but realized that some of the rafts with grandparents and young children needed their assistance much more. Minutes later, we were down the river, coasting calmly, admiring nature, and going over last minute instructions. I was still getting used to using the oar; as I flung it in the water, I noticed something in the woods.

I felt a warm sensation flow through my body. I lost myself in a trance, and the sunlight felt ten times heavier than usual. I was thankful to be surrounded by water. As I squinted and tried peering through the limbs to see what was watching me, I felt a small whack on top of my helmet. It was my dad hitting me with the oar, pointing my head forward towards the first rapid. "Oh shoot." I fumbled back in position and got ready for the journey. The cool reality shook chills down my spine.

The raft was divided front to back and left to right. Jim in back would call out who had to do what. And if one person was offbeat, the raft would spin, and the chance of us flipping skyrocketed. And if the raft is over-turned, the percentage of drowning also increases. I was not trying to get my foot stuck under a rock and die in two feet of raging water. Not today, so I did the best I could not to mess it up.

We conquered the first rapid and were geared up for the next couple. Bring it on Cucumber, Camel & Walrus, Eddy Turn, Dartmouth and Railroad Rapids! I felt invincible toward the loop but still had that weird feeling that I was still being surveyed from the riverbanks. I felt a blanket layer surrounding my body, but that vanished when I was splashed in the face by the Yough.

We paddled faster when Jim screamed go and held the oar firm in the water when we needed to turn. We were really getting the hang of it, and after a while Jim didn't even have to call out as much. We were working as one cohesive unit, and it felt good. We were not only one with each other on the raft, we were one with the rapids and river as well. My comfort ended where the water did, and that's right where we were heading.

Sketch of Juvie

We all pulled up to a riverside landing for lunch and a bathroom break. The river guides passed out sandwiches while others went swimming to cool off. I had to go pee really bad. I ran off into the woods, and almost immediately when I was out of sight from the group, a strange feeling swept over me. I was unfogging my glasses when I heard rustling from behind a tree. I almost pooped myself when a little kid jumped out from back there. He was all dirty. I turned my body to cover up and shook my head in confusion.

I gave up on that and went straight to the water. I jumped in and peed while pretending to cool off. I ate my sandwich in shame as I tried looking for that little kid's group. I couldn't find him anywhere, and he seemed to be too young to even be able to raft. My dad could tell something was up and asked me if anything was wrong. I told him some kid had spooked me in the woods. Phil and Nick came hustling back from the bathroom and said that some people had claimed to see a bear up there. Mazz explained that they probably eat the leftovers of lunch, and we all laughed.

It was time to hit the second half of the river run. There was one unnamed rapid before the famous Dimple Rock. We eased through that and came to a stop. The guides give the groups a choice between the deadly rapid and an alternate route. I looked to my dad, and he said, "This is why we are here." I took a deep breath and realized he was right.

Dimple Rock has an underground cave with no exit underneath. The strong current pulls you into the underwater cavern and never lets you leave. The rapid has claimed many lives in the past, but the rafting company does everything in their power to make it safe. They have a full crew of people on the rock and all surrounding areas with ropes, lifebelts, and Kisbee rings. If you hit the rock and flip, flow down the river and you will be safe. The real problem is when the raft gets caught up against the rock and basically swallows it beneath.

As we watched the groups successfully conquer the rapid, my confidence grew. But the raft just before us sent a shiver down my spine. The raft had a guide, grandchildren and elderly grandparents riding along. They were clearly fit but not ready for the violent strike that awaited them at Dimple Rock. They crashed and flipped into the raging waters. The entire crew flocked towards them, but luckily they had already passed the deadly hole.

After a bit of chaos and some mystery, we finally had the green light to go. I was relieved that I hadn't just witnessed an entire family perish right before my eyes. In that moment of clarity, I connected a few dots. I realized that the child I had seen in the woods was not on this rafting trip. Those kids we'd just watched flip were the youngest rafting. I remembered a joke from the safety meeting. That kid I had seen lived in those woods. And I think that bear that people saw was his mom.

I heard screaming, and we were approaching the rock. Jim was cussing me out, telling me to paddle! Phil splashed me with his oar. I was back. I dug into the river and straightened us out. But it was inevitable! We were going to hit the rock! Jim screamed, "Brace!" as we collided with the boulder. The raft rocked, but we did not flip. I felt a second chance at life but still felt a force from the river pulling me in. But I resisted with everything I had! I had my foot dug so deep into the bottom of the raft that I damn near hyperextended every part of my body, eluding doom. But we had survived.

We collectively exhaled and let out laughter when we were out of the monster's grasp. But the journey was still a long way from being finished. Ahead we had to face the famous Bottle of Wine and Double Hydraulic Rapids. Both known to be a vigorous dessert to Dimple Rock.

I wasn't too worried but had my ego checked. I watched my dad go overboard, and fear swept over me. I was trying to look back and see where he was floating, but I still had to paddle correctly and make sure that it wasn't going to be all of us pointing our toes in the water. It was much harder to control the winding raft with one less guy, but I had to step up.

I stabilized the barge, and we pulled off to the side, searching for my dad. Seconds felt like minutes, and minutes felt like hours. I desperately scanned the raging water and tried looking for hints from the river crew. I was looking for his helmet on the edge of the surface, and I was ready to jump right in to free him.

That strange feeling of being watched returned, but I didn't care. I think the other guys noticed as well because we continued downriver moments later. I really felt like I was giving up on my dad. I didn't want to leave; I didn't care if the "bear" got us. I needed to know my dad was alright.

I trembled down the river and was beginning to regret the entire trip. The harsh feeling evaporated when I heard Mazz laugh. Then Phil said, "There he is." My dad had been picked up by another group and had already made five new friends. I was relieved. We traded some snacks for our crew members and were off to finish the mission.

We hit Double Hydraulics, Rivers End and Schoolhouse Rapids and then took a swim in the river. It felt nice to stretch out and do the backstroke. I was sunburnt and exhausted. I laughed as the fish tickled my legs. This was what it was all about. Testing yourself so resting yourself feels incredible. We climbed back into the raft and started paddling as Nick made another "bear" joke.

We climbed Stairstep Rapid and prepared ourselves for Killer Falls. We were thrashed and thrown all around the lower Yough but still came out breathing and afloat. We finished Bruner Run and embraced each other, as we had finished the journey. We pulled into the landing and loaded the rafts onto the bus. I picked a window seat on the ride back. I kept my eyes peeled for one last look at our river stalker, but I drifted away asleep.

CHAPTER 4
WASHINGTON WILD THING
WASHINGTON, PENNSYLVANIA

Entering the portal

The Washington Wild Things were one of my favorite baseball teams growing up. They were an independent Minor League team that allowed you to get up close and personal with the game. My grandpa would take me out to the ballpark once or twice every summer, and we had many stories to tell. We have caught foul balls, gotten autographs, and even got to run on the field, but one night on our way home, something happened that I will never forget. We both got to see the creature that the local ball team was named after.

Mysterious monsters are no stranger to Appalachia. The eastern United States is filled with legends of snally-gaster, wampus cats, and werewolves. The native tribes and local townspeople both have serious warnings of staying away from the woods when the sun goes down. There have been many mysterious disappearances through the ages that have been linked to these unexplainable beasts.

Mountain Monsters filmed an episode in Washington County. They were hunting the Dustman, the most agile and fastest in the Appalachian Mountains. In 2019, a truck driver on Route 70 watched a "bear" dart across the road at mile marker 3. He said the creature ran on two legs and had a long snout like a dog. I believe my grandfather and I both witnessed the creature that these men were talking about, but we called it the wild thing.

After hitting Cabela's earlier in the day, Pepa and I drove to Washington for the baseball game. I peered out the window and pointed at the deer we spotted. There was always a bunch in the outfields of the baseball fields. We passed the park where they played the "Beast of the East" tournament... I wonder where they got that name.

We pulled past the mall and finally arrived at the

stadium. We parked in the gravel behind the field, and I always admired the house on the hill that could watch every game for free. We got our tickets, and I ran straight to the dugout. Pepa went to the concession stand, and by the time I would see him next, I had a baseball that was half full of autographs and was best friends with the mascot. The Wild Thing was some type of wildcat.

Washington Wild Thing mascot. Left to right: Me, Bart, Danny

The game started, and we had great seats. The Wild Things were playing the Miners, and we were out to an early lead. The pitcher threw a gem, so the game felt like it flew by. We had the game locked up going into the ninth, and we started heading toward the exit while still watching the final outs. They popped out to the infield, and we ran for the car to beat the rush.

We were westward, and I was ecstatic about the victory. I was gripping the laces on the ball, practicing different pitches and admiring the autographs, when my grandpa suddenly jerked to the left lane. I looked up and saw a deer angling right toward the road. I backed up in my seat and realized why it was on this suicidal path. The poor deer was being chased by this big black muscular wolf.

My grandpa was flooring it when he switched lanes. We had already been in a bad wreck when his Chevy Blazer rolled, and grandma's Buick was not ready for any dents. I turned my head back to see what happened to Bambi,, but she had leaped back into the darkness, and so did her pursuer. My stomach ached for the deer, but that's just the way of the forest.

My grandpa made a joke about that being a close one but seemed unfazed by the incident. He had seen many bears, mountain lions, and a plethora of other animals while hunting, so a wolf was nothing out of the ordinary. But I felt otherwise. The presence this creature held was unlike any animal in the wild. This animal knew what it wanted. It had a purpose. The wolf was using all four legs, but it looked similar to a human bear crawl. It may have been a werebear.

I asked my grandpa if he'd seen the wolf, and he shook his head. Of course he did. He'd probably spotted it well before me. After hunting for a half century and being a marine, he'd developed some keen skills. He mentioned that we have them that size on the farm as well. I wondered what he meant by that. Did he know this wolf was different? Were there lycanthropes lurking in Brock Ridge? The same creatures that King Arthur attempted to train? The pets that Adolph kept, maybe? Maybe that was what dropped from the trees on Jake and me... The offspring of the wild thing! The creature from the hieroglyphics!

CHAPTER 5
CLEAR LAKE CREATURE
ONTARIO, CANADA

Forest language and pathway

T he cottages at Clear Lake remind me of the Robin Williams movie *What Dreams May Come*. There is a heavenly explosion of color and expression flooding this campsite north of the SkyDome. The water is famous for the largemouth bass fishing and summertime activities. The unique coastline and immense marshlands provide a perfect home for beavers, deer, and other traveling animals. The Rideau waterway is rich in folklore and stories of aquatic monsters, but the locals told me a story of the best fisherman along the Ottawa... and he doesn't use a rod and reel.

There are thousands of Sasquatch sightings across Ontario and the rest of Canada. There are some communities that have been completely abandoned because they have been overrun by the creatures. The Nahanni Valley is infamous for red-eyed giants that have left many visitors beheaded. The people of Klemtu encounter these creatures on a daily basis.

Aboriginal tribes refer to the monsters as boqs, caddo critters, stinkahs, jacko, matlose, and yellow top. Saskatoon, Saskatchewan, is no stranger to the strangers. The country even had a bigfoot privy on the quarter next to Queen Elizabeth and the maple leaf. The kushtaka is an otterman known to save its victims before stealing their soul.

The wendigo is known to invade villages after long cold seasons when starvation is prominent. Natives who were forced to become cannibals were far more susceptible to possession of the beast. The show *Hannibal* is full of wendigo imagery and is obviously about cannibalism and primal instinct as well.

I have narrated many firsthand Canadian encounters. A ten-footer backed away from a tribesman wielding an axe next to a fire. A hiker saw a tall hulking figure from thirty meters during a solo hike in BC. A Pac West train worker is sadly plagued with nightmares after numerous encounters. There was a giant footprint found in 1991 on Vancouver Island, and a driver swerved to miss one more than a decade ago in Southern Ontario.

Sadly, a family in Port Alberni are being terrorized by creatures they believe to be related to *Gigantopithecus*. One first nation man named them Books; his village had many interactions with the yellers. He witnessed something spook a bear and force it to swim across the bay in an instant. A seismic outfit encountered a creature throwing rocks, making guttural sounds after being flown in deep north of Fort Nelson.

In Renfrew, a goose hunter had an encounter while he had some decoys in the water. He watched a monster man scooping water with his huge hands. After five minutes, his fishing bell went off, and the creature stared right at him. It ignored the bell completely. It growled a deep and guttural demonic growl and paralyzed him. He finally pulled his gun, and it ran off. It took him about twenty minutes to recover. He urged not to make eye contact with these beings; they have the ability to project fear.

In the summer of 2001, I skipped most of the baseball season for a once-in-a-lifetime fishing trip to Northern Ontario with my best friend's family. They had been renting at the cottages for years and had a community of friends who met back up every summer. I had heard many stories from Ian and his sisters about the lake and really couldn't wait to finally see the beautiful blue. My mom and grandpa were excited that I was getting to visit some uncharted waters and sent me along with some lucky lures. My dad dropped me off at the Colemans' and asked me to get him an Argonauts shirt.

I loaded my stuff into Ian's car and went into the house for dinner. Ian was playing N64 while the twins were finishing packing up when Mrs. Coleman invited me to sit down for chicken and potatoes, her signature dish. She was staying home to take care of the animals but had been up to the cottages plenty of times. She was excited for me to meet her people and finally see what all the fuss was about. She told me to take the paddleboat out to bass cove for some huge largemouth. She put her hand on my hand and looked me in the eye and asked me not to let Ian go to Misty Island. And before I got to ask, the entire family poured into the kitchen, and it was just about time to go.

We drove through the night, and I was in the back with the twins. They were making fun of me because I had never water-skied before. The girls said I might have to stick to the kneeboard. Whatever that meant... They were talking trash about shuffleboard and horseshoes too, but at least we would all be on the same team in the USA versus Team Canada soccer match... The girls didn't care to fish much though... "Not anymore," they said.

A few hours later we were at the famous duty-free

shop on the Canadian border. I was out of the country for the first time, if the Lake Erie boat trips didn't officially count. We met up with a family that was friends with the Colemans, the Moviels. I knew them through St. Eds, my dad's alma mater. The brothers later went on to play for the Mariners and Mets, for now we were Cleveland brothers in Canadian territory.

Wildman track

The Coleman clan fell asleep in the back while I rode in the front with Rich. He was the coach of the peewee Falcons and actually had drafted me, but I was already playing with the Browns because they were family. He told me I would have my own room, pointed out the buildings of downtown Toronto, and told me all about the species of fish in the lake system. He said we had to watch out for wolves and black bear. I asked him if that was what scared the twins, and he replied, "The thing that scared the girls scares the bear too."

The clan must have felt a familiar turn because they all woke up, and moments later we were pulling into the cottages. It was a magical feeling arriving while the birds were chirping. I ran around following Ian while he pointed out all the hotspots. He showed me the shuffle-board courts, the paddleboats, and where they displayed the nightly movie. We greeted the fishermen and found the girls on the beach. We unpacked in the cozy cabin, and it was time for breakfast!

We devoured breakfast and met the rest of Ian's crew. One big kid called himself Karp, and his two cousins were named Rod and Hook. Clearly they came from a fisherman family. They gave us a tour of their cabin, freezer and also their tackle box. They knew all the best spots around the waterway. They were the true kings of the summer.

Ian was excited to show me bass cove. We rented a paddleboat and got our reels ready. We crossed the misty waters into a mysterious lagoon. We dropped our lines in, and boom, we had them snagged. Giant bass went after our worms within seconds. We caught and released some cows. I've never seen such active waters.

We were having such a blast and lost track of time. We were out there for hours, but it only felt like minutes. We were so busy unhooking and baiting our lines, we failed to notice the dark clouds approaching. After a while we finally saw the storm approaching but chose to ignore it. The fishing was too good, and I was worried I'd never have that luck again. I was right.

We told each other one more catch and agreed. Rain was now falling, and the waves were beginning to grow. We were stubborn and kept fishing. Thirty minutes later, it was a downpour, but we were still catching fish. We heard a tree crash toward the bank, and we figured it was the storm telling us to go.

We both stared toward the sound and continued to fish. Then another tree fell. That one was not the wind. Ian knew exactly what it was and murmured, "We have to go," under his breath. As we packed up the boat and started pedaling, there was a roar of thunder from the sky and an even bigger one from the treeline. I was too scared to even turn around. I knew it was a monster, but I think he was trying to help us. I was taking his advice and getting home.

We made it to the marina just by the time the weather was getting ugly. Waves were forming, and rain was pouring down sideways. We ran into cover with our hands full and hearts still pumping from our lagoon encounter. Ian's dad laughed as we barreled into the cabin soaking wet. He asked us how it went and replied, "You see it?" while smiling. Ian was still shaking, and his dad knew we had encountered the creature.

I took a warm shower and changed clothes in my room. By the time I climbed out for lunch, the twin sisters had heard about our lagoon encounter. They came into my room and asked me if I got a visual. I told them that I didn't see too much but could sure feel the monster in my chest. They told me they had been lost in the lagoon years ago and had heard loud screams with trees crashing down. Becca swore she'd seen the monster through the branches. They were afraid he was going to sink their boat, but I truly think it's the exact opposite. He warns people of getting too close to his island. He might be our buffer to a much meaner creature.

The rest of the week flew by. I made a bunch of friends, and those times felt like they would last forever. We made plans for the next summer and promised to keep in touch, but sadly, I never spoke to my Canadian friends again. I hope one day on our journey, our destined paths will intertwine once again. I am forever grateful for that sea monster. If we had stayed out there on those choppy waters for much longer, our boat would have capsized, and we most likely would have drowned. Nobody would have heard us screaming.

CHAPTER 6
SUSQUEHANNA SEAL
COOPERSTOWN, NEW YORK

My sister and I at Cleveland Zoo

The Susquehanna River is a summertime paradise away from the chaos of the big city in New York. Abundant in resources, the "oyster river" begins at Otsego Lake in Cooperstown and flows all the way down to Chesapeake Bay. The water played an important role in the discovery of the state of Pennsylvania, but what's lurking below the surface might be even more interesting.

According to Indian legend and later confirmed by discoveries during excavations in the 1900s, there were once giants who roamed these lands... and some had horns. But the legend doesn't stop at bones, there have been many recent sightings of mysterious creatures along one of the oldest rivers of the world. The wendigo suffers from starvation no matter how much meat it consumes. Some would say it's a mercy to kill one because living with the wendigo appetite is worse than dancing with the devil himself. And his tune will never end.

In Celtic mythology, selkie folk are seals that can become human. In Scotland, the seals shed their skin and became beautiful humans. The sealskin holds magical abilities to shapeshift. Without the skin, the being is unable to transform. There are many stories of human and selkie encounters. One man was drowning and doomed, when his wife turned back into a seal and thankfully rescued him. Other men tried stealing the sealskin for themselves, only furthering the distance between the two races.

Many witnesses compare the Susquehanna Seal to the feared cryptid down under, the bunyip. Bunyip translates to devil and evil spirit. The water-dwelling monster lurks in swamps, billabongs, riverbeds, and waterholes. The creature is known for hunting humans and large animals. They love the taste of children, women, and foreigners. They are said to have tusks, feathers, claws, scales, horns, and supernatural powers. Aboriginal tribes avoided riverbanks and night walks. There are many children's books and at least nine different tribal variations of the mythical creature.

Newspapers reported the bunyip had the head of a crocodile, dark fur and the tail of a horse. Other witnesses claim the tail is serrated like the tail of a stingray. They have flippers and evil conniving eyes. Some tribes describe an aggressive one-eyed creature with a mouth on its stomach. There have been bones and skeletons found deep in caves that led to multiple declarations of the bunyip being an undiscovered, living, breathing animal. Sightings to this day are still piling up in the Baggy Greens.

When I was twelve, my family visited Cooperstown for the Dreams Park baseball tournament. We were one of the best teams in the state of Ohio and were invited to play in the famous international bracket. I was excited to see the Hall of Fame and compete against some of the best in the world. I had heard many stories over the years about the park, so I was itching the entire six-hour drive from Cleveland.

Dreams Park has a chapter of its own in my *Haunted Camps and Campuses* book, but this one focuses on our day away from the baseball fields. My family picked me up from the park for a day on the river. We visited the Zorijes, who were staying at an awesome riverfront rental. There were waterslides and trampolines, so basically we were in childhood heaven. I was more trying to fish than get in the water, but I wasn't going to be the only dry one.

I was hesitant jumping in the dark water because I knew what could be lurking below. I knew large snakes and giant catfish were not far from my dangling legs. Plus we had heard from lifeguards that there were bull sharks in the Otsego Lake. And that flowed right down into these waters. I kept my eyes open for fins and anything else that looked out of place.

As time went by, I grew a little more comfortable in the murky waters. I knew the monsters were near, but they must have been used to coexisting with humans in these stretches. We wrestled on the trampoline and threw each other off the side of the slide. Then we started jumping off the high slide and catching the football diving into the water. After a couple of throws, I climbed up for my time to play receiver.

I climbed up the slide and rubbed my eyes to help see better without my glasses. As the shadows cleared, I saw something swimming toward the bank in the distance. It looked like a beaver. I smiled and tried to get a better look. By that time, the younger Zorijes were growing impatient and yelling at me to hurry up.

I noticed the beaver was just the creature's head. And it started to rise out of the water. I really wished I had my glasses, but I could tell this thing was big. I wondered if it was a diver but couldn't see a snorkel. I heard the guys calling, but I ignored them. Then smack, the football drilled me in the side of my head. I fell into the water with my ear bleeding and ringing. Concussed.

Next thing I knew, I was being pulled out of the river, and all the parents were surrounding me. First thing I asked when I came back to life was "Did you see that thing?" They had no clue what I was talking about and just thought it was the head trauma speaking. My mom put my glasses on me, and I rushed back to the river. I pointed toward the bank and said, "I saw something right there!"

Sketch of the Susquehanna Seal

Alex believed me. He could tell I had been distracted by something on the top of the slide. He knew I wouldn't just ignore everyone screaming for no reason. They were the ones ignoring what I was looking at. He asked me what I thought it was. I told him at first I thought it was a beaver; then I noticed it was the size of a man. His eyes lit up. He had encountered a creature near his house at Sleepy Hollow. He asked if it was the wolfman, and I replied more like the Gill-man.

We decided to adventure and look for clues along the trail by the river. By that time, all Alex's brothers were interested in the hunt. My sister joined along as well. They had all heard of the wolfman and stuck very close to us.

We approached the bank where I had spotted the creature. The entire area smelled like dead fish. There were weird slide marks in the mud but nothing we could identify. Flies were buzzing violently as Michael called us over to a pit. There were hundreds of fish carcasses and bones everywhere. It was an eerie sight. We backed off slowly and heard a call from the river. It was some old fisherman.

He pulled his little metal boat to the bank and asked us what we were doing. I told him we were just hiking the trail and looking for worms. He asked, "What's that God-awful smell?" and before I could make an excuse, Mike led him to the pit. The man was stunned and went right back to his boat. He told us to get home and to keep quiet. Erin asked him, "Keep quiet about what?" He scanned all of our faces and in a dead serious voice replied, "The river demon."

We wandered back to the house and joined our parents around the fire. We did the opposite of what the fisherman said and asked the adults about the "water demon". They brushed it off and said the old man was just trying to scare us. Then Mike said, "We found its den!" Then Alex shouted, "And Connor saw it!" My parents beamed at me!

"I thought it was a beaver." And the moms quickly replied, "Then it probably was!" And then I continued, saying, "It started to stand up out of the water." They quickly shushed me and said that I was seeing things due to my concussion. My sister was quick to point out that I had spotted the creature before my head was caved in. The parents made sure we didn't leave their sight the rest of the night.

As the sun went down and the skies got darker, we heard the chorus of frogs and crickets reigning through the river. Then like the mute button got pressed, the surrounding area went completely dead. The silence was deafening. The stillness came to a halt when we heard strange groans and splashing toward the pit. Mike said, "He's feasting," and I pictured the beast devouring large fish and disposing of their heads in that pile of flies.

The adults ushered us inside, and the night came to an end shortly after. The next day we returned to Dreams Park for more baseball. After the tournament, the team went to Otsego Lake for our final team picnic. The story of the river demon came to the surface, and some locals overheard us talking about it. They came over to us and said that the creature we encountered was called the Susquehanna Seal. Others named it the West Branch Dugong. I was relieved to hear that others had experienced this creature. They warned us that we were very lucky to survive the encounter.

After hearing about the Susquehanna Seal, the blurry image of what I saw began to take shape in my mind. The creature I saw was long, slender and grayish black like a dolphin. It seemed to be a blend of marine animal and hominid species. After watching *Creature from the Black Lagoon*, I felt the animal that I had encountered was similar to the Gill-man. I am very lucky that I didn't meet the same fate as the characters on that scientific journey.

CHAPTER 7
TENNESSEE TITANS
APPALACHIAN MOUNTAINS

Look and Tremble

M y friend's favorite team is the Tennessee Titans, but he doesn't believe in bigfoot. That's like a Christian who doesn't believe in God. Okay, maybe not that far, but after you hike the Smoky Mountains, if you still believe we are the only ones out there, I'll buy the tickets for the next game. There have been mysterious disappearances and decades of firsthand encounters that paint a clear picture of why the football team got their name, I can assure you of that.

There have been encounters in the Appalachian Mountains that go back to the day of the mound builders, but the Nephilim descendants have still been spotted to this day. The natives hunted alongside the friendly giant clans and competed with the territorial ones. They were referred to as yahoo, stonish giants, and raven mockers. There are small species similar to Aipom that have been reported as well.

In Mary Green's book *50 Years with Bigfoot*, she documented the interesting relationship between the Carter family and a clan of Sasquatch on their Tennessee farm. Mary was a pioneer in the community and sadly was killed for digging too deep. I believe she was murdered because these secrets are detrimental to the web of control.

One evening, the grandfather had found a baby bigfoot that had been badly injured and pinned down by a fallen tree. He freed it and brought the little guy home to dress his wounds. Carter thought he was a neighbor's deformed son and kept him in his home while asking around. After no answers and the boy trashing the inside of his home, he built him an outside stall and named him Fox. A few nights later, he heard a loud crack in the night and saw two adult bigfoots breaking the wood and freeing the juvenile.

Weeks later, he noticed the child would follow him in the treeline while Roberts worked on the farm. The parents had migrated, and Fox stayed at the farm. Over time, the two formed a rare bond that could only happen how it happened. Carter spoke six Native American languages and was able to communicate with Fox. Every night after dinner, Grandpa would bring food to the barn and work with Fox.

Strange creature caught on security camera

Janice and Lila were the granddaughters of the Carter family. They both met with Mary Green on the property and explained everything they knew about their family's relationship with these creatures. They explained that Fox grew up and met Sheba. Together they had near ten children. The men would leave the territory to find a mate when they became of age. And the women took care of the young until a male bigfoot came to mate when they matured.

Robert and Fox introduced their families to each other over time. Sheba was hesitant around humans but never let go of a pink quilt they gifted her. Janice held hands with Fox and his young children. They played together near the creek and ate mud pies. Over time, both groups grew to trust one another, but there were still some barriers between the two human species.

She grew up with one named Blackie but had a bad feeling about him. He made lewd gestures toward her and was very aggressive. Years later, he kidnapped a girl and abused her. A nearby farmer heard her screams and luckily saved her. The girl spent the rest of her life in an institution, scarred from the incident. Janice was sad to say that it could have been her or baby sister. Another time Sheba knocked Janice off her horse, but those were the only threatening times.

Fox and Robert shared fishing and hunting techniques. The family would find dead animals up in the trees, tower stacks of slate rocks along the creeks, and limbs in teepee formations. Janice learned some of Fox's language and wrote it in a notebook. *Pena* meant sugar, *pah-mo* was a word for smoke, and they called the sun *Nanica*. The cows were *potsane*, dogs were *habbe*, owl was *mope*, and *nawk* meant friend. *Gway* meant now, and *geam* meant love. Their friendship broke barriers known to most men.

When Grandpa got older, Fox would visit him near the porch. He would sleep in the cellar when it would get cold. He broke open all the canned foods one winter when Robert didn't feed them. The family had plaster casts of Fox's daughter Nicki and her mate, Bo. They often found scat and animal bones on the farm's property. Fox visited Robert often in his final days and knew the end was near. They were best friends.

Years later, when Janice and Lila came back to the property, they rarely saw Fox but could still feel that he was out there. When Mary Green was visiting the farm, an older gray bigfoot was captured on camera, keeping a close eye on the group from the wood line. This was the last we heard of Fox. May this bond forever be remembered. This footage was broken down by Scott Carpenter, another Tennessee man with an interesting relationship with bigfoot.

Scott has written multiple books on Sasquatch and has even worked on DNA genome projects. He has captured countless encounters and faces on his hiking camera. He has had bigfoot follow him home for over fifty miles. They have left gifts and been spotted by his neighbors. Scott is Christian based and believes they are children of the watchers. He has rebuked the Nephilim from his property, but they still follow him every time he hits the trail.

Sadly, not everyone escapes unharmed. There have been many people who have vanished from the Appalachian Mountains and in particular the Great Smoky Mountain National Park. Rangers have been attacked and are well aware of other forces that lurk in the protected lands. In 1969, tragedy struck when a young boy vanished while camping during Father's Day weekend that changed the Tennessee landscape forever.

Small indentation

Dennis Martin was six years old when he disappeared at Spence Field in 1969. He was camping with his older brother and dad on June 14. Another family, also named the Martins, arrived with two sons as well. The four boys were playing hide-and-seek and wanted to prank the parents. The boys were going to hide on each side of the trail and jump scare the adults. Dennis was wearing a bright red sweatshirt, so he was told to go to the other side of the trail. That was the last time Dennis was seen, well, maybe.

The Key family was nearby at Rowan's Creek, searching for bears, when they were startled by something in the woods. They heard a ferocious shriek and saw a large hairy being in the woods. They said it was an unkept giant man. The Keys also mentioned that the creature had something flung over its shoulder. And that thing was red. The FBI quickly said the incident was not connected to the disappearance and swept it under the rug. Mr. Martin was furious when he later found out about the encounter from the newspaper. He made the hike himself and proved that the trek was clearly possible.

When the record-breaking search party arrived, so did the storms. There were torrential downpours for the next three days that wiped away any evidence that could have been possibly found. The search and rescue workers then witnessed the Green Berets arrive. The park was then emptied while the jungle fighters arrived for their mission.

Dennis Martin's body was never found. A footprint

of a shoe similar to Denny's was located but ultimately led to nothing. A ginseng hunter claimed to find a boy's skull but waited twenty years to report it due to fear of being arrested for illegal activity. No more leads were ever officially documented, but many locals claim to know what happened to the boy.

The locals know that Dennis wasn't the only one. Many children have been taken from the Smokies. And many local families had no choice but to fight back. Other hunting groups were employed to take care of the problem. Elite marksmen and trackers were hired to exterminate the wild people. This was what the Green Berets had been brought in to do. The creatures had broken the treaty, and it was time for them to pay.

Sadly, there have been bad things done by both sides, and many innocent lives were lost. The FBI official who was overseeing the Dennis Martin case ended up committing suicide shortly after the search was called off. Many say that he could not live with himself after he saw what the Green Berets pulled out of the forest. The soldiers killed many women and children and Sasquatches that were sadly collateral damage in this horrible situation. I truly wish there were more stories like the Carter family and less Missing 411 cases around the world.

In January 2013, Bird and I were driving from Cleveland down to Orlando to do video work for the USFTL National Flag Football Championships. It was over a thousand miles and sixteen hours of road time at best.

We left in the evening and heard warnings of a bad snowstorm in the mountains. We took the turnpike, 77 South, and it was known to be dangerous even in the best of conditions. We kept an eye out for deer while talking for hours. Time flew by. My radio suddenly turned on, and we laughed that we had been talking nonstop for a good six hours without it. We relaxed to some music while going the speed limit. The snow was thick, and each turn had a cliff side of hundreds of feet. We were definitely ready for the Florida sunshine. This was our escape every January from the cold.

Tennessee vs. Jaguars…Go Titans!!!!

After a while of zoning out focused on the road, in Southern West Virginia near the Tennessee border, we both jolted up, pointing, saying did you see that?! We both had seen the same thing. A giant figure stepping down a bank from a very large tree on the right side of the road. It disappeared into the darkness as we approached with our headlights.

I slowed down a bit to look back, but we both knew we couldn't get far in the snow, and it wouldn't be safe for other cars approaching. The adrenaline sure woke us up, but we both knew it was time to get off the road. There wasn't a rest stop for many miles, so we had to find a place to stop for the night. We were both dozing off, and luckily I found a pull-off where a few semi-trucks had set up for overnight. We pulled up between them, shut the car off and bundled up.

Before we fell asleep, we joked about what we had seen. It was either a giant, a bigfoot or a walking tree. We laughed, but I was nervous about sleeping so close to the wood line. Bird was more worried about the cold. He reminded me of the stories that he'd told me growing up about the wolfman. I fell asleep and woke up with my teeth chattering. I luckily got the car started up and was back on the road. A few hours later there was sunshine and swampland. Years later, I still have dreams and visions of that snowy night in the Appalachian Mountains.

CHAPTER 8
FLORIDA SKUNK APE
GREEN SWAMP, FLORIDA

Skunk ape evidence

M any people think Florida is just Disney castles and spring break beaches, but most of the state is farms, swampland and trailer parks. While Florida Man stays in the spotlight, the skunk ape enjoys creeping in the shadows. The swamp thing has been spotted on the saltwater coasts and deep in the bayou since the Seminole days, but when a woman photographed a large one eating apples in her backyard in Myakka, the state woke up. From the Everglades to Ocala, you must watch out for snakes, gators, and jaguar, but most of all, the skunk ape.

Most people believe the monster gets its name from the god-awful smell that lingers with every big step, but that's not the only root. In the 1940s in the northern Panhandle, there was a large Sasquatch that had a white stripe down his head and back like a skunk. The local people who encountered the wild man coined him the skunk ape, but others call 'em stump jumpers, swamp things, cabbage man, mango people, and many other names in those moments of their world being turned upside down and shook out.

After about eight months that I was living in Lakeland, my mom moved down to the Panhandle. It was about five and a half hours away, and I would make the drive quite often. I'd drive by the *Jeepers Creepers* locations in Ocala, see the gators in Gainesville and the Noles in Tally, but I always feared driving through the Green Swamp. Near Colt Creek State Park, you lose all cell reception and are at least fifty miles from any help.

I left Calhoun County around ten so I could drive through the night and miss the crazy Florida traffic. I crossed the time zone and looked over the Apalachicola River bridge, admiring the swamps below, and was off again to the Biltmore in Lakeland. A few hours later, I passed Lake City and was heading south toward oblivion. I texted my mom that I was near Colt Creek before turning my busted phone on airplane mode entering the Green Swamp.

Left to right: Robert Robinson, Dave Sidoti, me, Stacy Brown Jr.

I turned my brights on and kept my eyes open for deer, cops and debris in the road. I heard stories of killer hitchhikers, giant panthers, and of course stories of the

swamp thing. The creek was known for haunted abandoned homesteads, large gators and old Indian tales of
the supernatural. I was limited on gas, so I set cruise
control, I sparked up a joint, and then I suddenly saw
something ahead.

I locked my doors and turned off my music. I saw a
figure in the middle of the road. The shadow was waving
their arms, and I had to give my eyes a rub. A car was
pulled off on the side. I couldn't believe it; I thought I
was getting set up. It was a woman, and she looked like
she needed help.

I pulled off to the side of the road, and she came
running to my car. She said that her tire popped, and she
couldn't put her spare on. I was relieved and said that I
could help. She stopped me and said she knew how, but
just couldn't. I said that maybe my equipment would
work and popped my trunk. She slammed my trunk
down and said, "No! I can't cuz somethings out there!"
while pointing toward the woods. I asked her if it was a
man, bear, or what. She said it was a werewolf; she said
it growled at her.

I figured it was just an angry panther and popped my
trunk again. I gave her a flashlight and told her to give
me some light, but she kept shining it towards the
woods. Maybe it was a rabid 'yote. After a few minutes, I
had the car jacked up and the tire just about off when I
heard some shuffling in the treeline. I didn't pay much
attention until my workplace went completely dark. She

was frozen in fear and shining the light towards the noise.

When I finally looked toward her eyes' gaze, I was deeply startled. I saw a large shadow figure just beyond the treeline. The bog man was fascinated by the pretty woman. I dropped the tools, and the monster finally broke his stare. He turned his head slightly towards me and was unhappy that I was disrupting his night with his Ann Darrow.

At Dave Shealy's Skunk Ape Headquarters in the Everglades

Seconds felt like hours. I was hit by waves of energy that I couldn't even understand. He let out a ferocious roar and took off into the thicket. We could hear him breaking branches and shaking the ground, still screaming. It felt like all the air from the area left with him. I gasped for breath.

Without hesitation, she ran toward my car and demanded we go! She hopped in the back and was silent for a while. After a few minutes of confusion, she asked, "Where's your passenger seat?" and we both busted out laughing. She said, "I told you it wasn't a panther." I said, "That was no werewolf either, that was a Sasquatch!" She yelled, "The skunk ape!"

We made it to town and pulled into the gas station. I was filling up when a sheriff pulled in behind me. The woman ran over to him and told her story. He approached me, and I was a bit nervous. He thanked me and said I might have saved her life out there. There had been many sightings in that stretch, and some of the encounters were quite aggressive.

The pretty woman ran over to me and gave me a hug. She said the sheriff would drive her back to her car, and she was very thankful that I had showed up. She offered me money for my lost tools, but I was not worried about it. I told her good luck on her journey and was back off into the night. I was glad I pulled over and didn't just keep driving. I didn't need that on my conscience.

CHAPTER 9
OCHEESEE POND WILD MAN
CALHOUN COUNTY, FLORIDA

In the late 1800s, a large feral man of the shadows was wreaking havoc on a small swamp village not far from Black Lagoon. The creature of the dark was terrorizing children, killing livestock and hurling out bloodcurdling screams in the night. A group of hunters and soldiers tracked the monster and captured the wild man deep in the cypress. They believed he was an escaped mental patient, and he was sent to the state hospital. He died a few years later, but his descendants have been spotted many times over the last century.

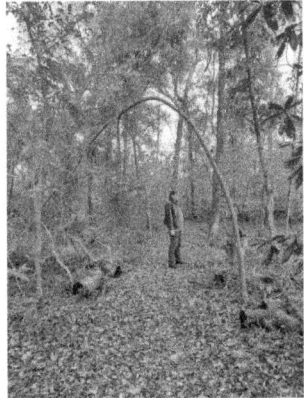

My good friend, Ninja looking for the Wild Man

In October 2018, right after Hurricane Michael ripped

our region apart, I had some strange occurrences in my Panhandle trailer. There were trees and debris sprawled in every direction. My windows were broken, and the outside sheeting and skirting were miles away. We didn't have power for twenty-six days (and we were one of the lucky ones); the nights were dark, hot and silent.

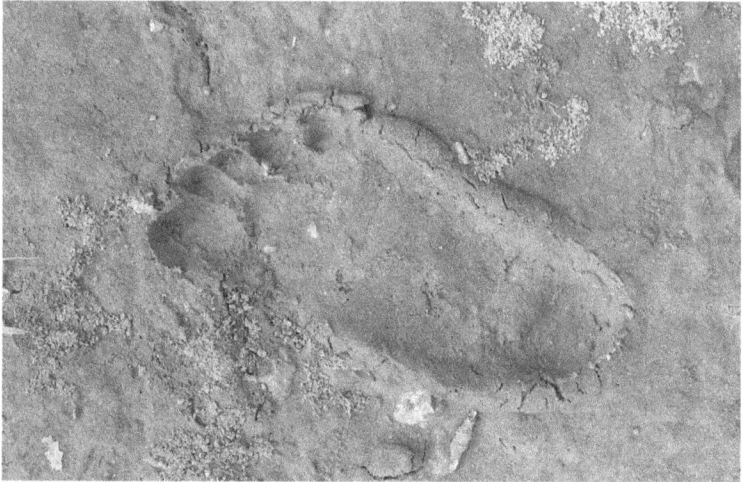

Ocheesee Pond track discovered by my mom

The first few nights after the storm I had trouble sleeping. The loud crashes and thrashes from the hurricane would return, and I would roll over in my bed. The human body was never supposed to experience something so intense. I truly felt sorry for those in war. The night terrors and roaring skies pummeled me into submission. It crossed my mind that moving down south may have been a mistake. The soil was stained, and we were all scarred.

The cries of my mother watching all her fruit trees tumble over in her newly acquired dream home really stung. But luckily I evacuated my trailer and made it over to her sturdy home. One of my neighbors was rolled over, and another roof was ripped off. I'm glad we were safe, but the trauma was still very real. My heart goes out to the more than seventy people who were killed by Michael.

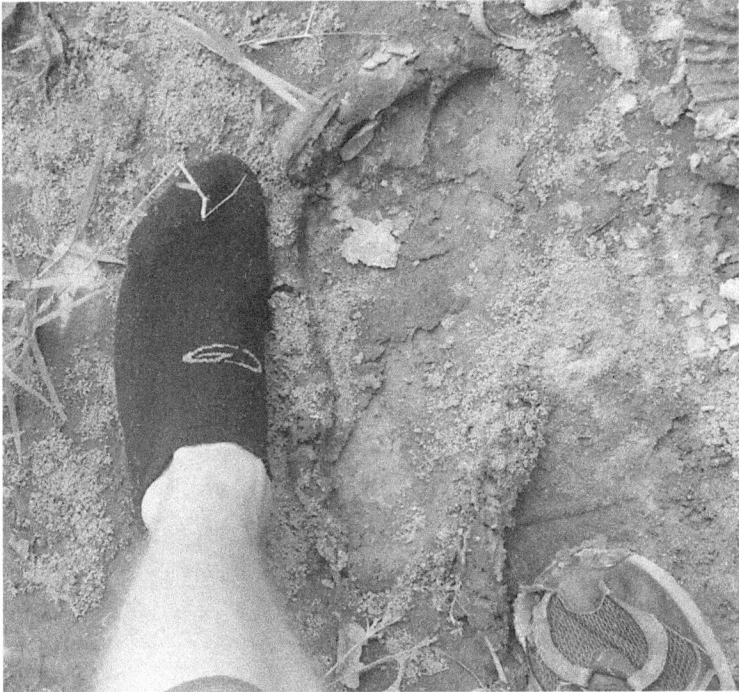

My foot next to another track of the Ocheesee Pond Wild Man

In the middle of the night during the blackout, I'd

feel a banging on the sides of my single-wide. It was loud and vibrated the entire frame. It would wake me up and stir my cats up, but most of the time I'd just fall right back asleep. It happened five or six times. It felt like a dream, but most of the day did as well. We were surrounded by debris and split trees. It begins to play tricks on the mind. I couldn't tell if something was targeting my trailer or if it was PTSD.

One night, it was strong enough to get me to peek out the window. I looked outside and to my surprise caught a glimpse of a large white blur and some wild dogs running barking off toward the woods. I scribbled "FL heard something late night 3 a.m., looked out the window, saw something white/big" in my journal and went back to sleep.

Playing a Bigfoot hunter in Nimrods in Fall

Another hunter in the area told me that activity had picked up right after the storm as well. He and his neighbor heard loud trampling and a path being cleared through the fallen trees. I sure hope they sensed the storm and found safety. But that weird window of a couple of days after a natural disaster could have cryptids, creatures and the common folk on the same path of survival.

My friend Ronnie has been hiking these creeks for decades now and has had many encounters with the creature. He was lucky enough to find a thumb bone of a giant. The first metacarpal bone was almost bigger than my entire thumb. The petrified fossil was very heavy in my hand. He also found a shoulder blade deep in the clay. Remnants surround us.

I had a recent encounter about thirty miles from the pond with the stump jumper. June 5, my friend and I did a nighttime hike for the eclipse. My companion Ronnie is former military and a lifetime hunter and tracker. We adventured to Bellamy Bridge, which was known to be a paranormal hotspot. The hike is short but creepy at nighttime. A blanket of mist covers the path and Chipola River swamps. We were out there for a few hours.

We told scary stories, meditated, and just listened to the words of the forest. We were talking about the swamp thing and heard a loud hooting call from the distance. It stopped us in our conversation's tracks and rumbled our chests. I have it recorded on my go pro camera. Ronnie tried calling back but was met with no response. It was either an owl or a warning from a wild man. There was a blanket of strange vibrations sprawled out through the dark forest.

It was very eerie because it only hooted one time. I was well aware that both linked to ancient legends and Missing 411. For the next forty-five minutes, we watched glowing orbs in the sky. It looked similar to heat lightning but was just above the tree canopy. In the surrounding forest, an eerie feeling spread around the end of the trail. We knew something was nearby, and it was confirmed when we heard a large tree crash about thirty yards from us. My GoPro burned out minutes before it. Not a dead battery, it just got so hot it turned off. Strange, could be the old batteries finally going bad, or it was infrasound...

I was terrified after that crashing tree. I could feel it in my sternum. I envisioned rillaboom attacking. I armed myself with my knife, and Ronnie had his hand on his protector. He joked he wished he'd brought his bigger one. I wished I had one. My toothpick wouldn't stop anything from snapping me in half. We did not want to hurt whatever it was, but we were ready to protect ourselves.

We stayed out there another hour with minimal activity. Sometimes the entire forest would go silent and get darker even with the full moon eclipse going on. The vibes were definitely a little spooky. Especially with what's going on in the world and the people in charge finally releasing those authentic UFO videos proving there are unknown and supernatural forces at play every day. But that is ancient knowledge, of course.

Another time near Look and Tremble Rapids, I was with my neighbor and his son, hanging out along the Chipola. We recorded videos talking about the Seminole legends, monster gators, and religious snake handlers who passed away back here. We enjoyed the white water and skipped rocks.

We did some tree knocks, and the kid did some bigfoot calls. Right after one of his hoots, a tree branch fell. The nearby forest went silent, and we didn't stick around much longer after that. We are always searching for signs when we are out there.

CHAPTER 10
HONEY ISLAND SWAMP MONSTER

PEARL RIVER, LOUISIANA

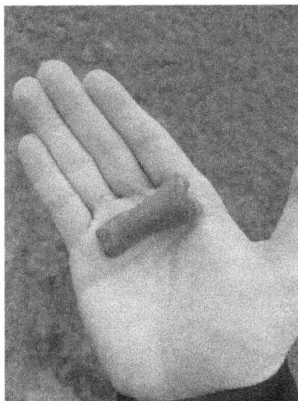
Fossil from extinct animal

The Honey Island Swamp is a true paradise for reptilians and mammals alike. Runaway circuses, Indian burial mounds and piles of hidden treasure saturate the Spanish moss of the bayou. Aggressive gators, angry hogs and enormous snakes patrol the perimeter grounds while the simple-life fishermen just catch enough fish to survive. On the edge of the space test zone, it's not surprising that there have been some strange creatures spotted in the water. The most famous is the three-toed swamp thing, the Honey Island Swamp monster!

According to Cajun legend, when someone skips Lent for seven years straight, they become cursed. For 101 nights, they will be transformed into the rougarou. The half man hybrid beast will have the taste for blood and a thirst that can never be quenched. Other reports say that a circus crashed, and the chimpanzees mated with the crocodiles. This beast is even more dangerous than Reverend Zombie and the Bayou Butcher.

The legend of Victor Crowley is told in the four Hatchet movies. Victor's father cheated on his dying wife with the family nurse. Their unborn child was placed under a voodoo spell. Victor was born deformed and mutated. Thomas raised him in the Honey Island Swamp on the outskirts of existence. One day a group of teenagers lit their cabin on fire with Victor inside. Vic tragically died, and his spirit was trapped in time. He was resurrected and killed anybody who visited his haunted swamp.

After a misunderstanding left me on the Biloxi streets for the night, I bathed on the beach by the loop and looked for shark teeth. I found some cool rocks and jelly-fish but no megalodon fossils. I dried off and called the Honey Island Swamp tours and booked a spot on their two-hour boat tour. I was excited to finally check the swamp off my bucket list.

As I drove westward, I reminisced on the last few times I'd visited New Orleans. We had memorable stays with interesting people. Our friend Jana was born in China and raised as a cave diver. She has lived all over the world and is now the leader of an important Mardi Gras group. The other guy we stayed with was ex-military and a bike deliveryman. He has ridden across America on two-wheelers that he built himself. Both our friends had stories for days.

Honey Island Swamp tour

The guy was a big NASA fan. However, I am not. He wanted to strangle me when I told him the Earth was a flat plane and that NASA means to deceive in Ancient Hebrew. I chuckled about it as I entered the space testing zone. No wonder there are deformed monsters in the swamp. It's just like *The Hills Have Eyes* out there.

I was getting close and passed the rest stop we'd slept at years before. I remember setting up on the ground just outside the car because there was barely any room with five of us packed tight in the small SUV. I fell asleep quickly but was woken up in the middle of the night by something making a ruckus in the treeline. I crawled back in the car and pissed everyone off when I woke them up. Better pissed off than pissed on.

I pulled off the Slidell exit and had my eyes peeled for gators, creatures and even aliens! The movie *Midnight Special* was filmed right here and many other places along the Emerald Coast. I was right where I needed to be. I followed the signs and took the winding dirt roads to the cabin. I ripped my cart and was ready to go.

I bought a hat, koozie, gator claws, and a bunch of postcards from the gift shop. I figured it would be cool memorabilia and presents for my cryptid family. I marveled at the crayon drawings of the Honey Island Swamp monster. And of course I had to ask the guy at the front desk if he'd had any encounters. He shook his head no but said his grandfather had shot one of them. He said the scariest thing in the swamp is the quicksand. I laughed but trembled when I imagined being sucked underground by the sand.

Before I knew it, I was on the boat and sitting through the safety guidelines. There was no standing up, no smoking, and no reaching over the edge. He didn't have to say that twice. The giant gators reminded everyone very quickly that we were safest sitting back and enjoying the view. Our captain also warned, "And if we run into the rougarou, do not stare into its eyes."

We covered about thirteen miles on the high-speed pontoon boat. He pointed out the interesting riverside homesteads and asked us how many boatloads of materials it took to build each of them. We fed marshmallows to alligators and visited the magic tree from *The Princess and the Frog*. We were infiltrated by snakes! They rained down from the trees!

After our reptilian encounter, we spotted something very strange up the river ahead. We slowed down to get a better look; a nauseating odor swept the air. The baby on the boat started to cry, and most of the people were covering their nose. The captain didn't get too close. I had my eyes locked on the surface and in the woods behind, scanning for clues.

There was a light brown bloated carcass floating toward the shoreline. I could see a long snout and strange wrinkles. At first glance, I thought it was a deer that had filled up with fluid, but the captain said it was an alligator. I'm not sure I agree with him. There were no scales, and it was not the greenish tint that most gators appear. Cap, of course, was on the water far more than me, but I think he didn't want to raise panic amongst the families. I snapped a few pictures before we jetted off. The boat was under a spell.

The creature looked like it came from *Silent Hill* or

Resident Evil. It reminded me of the zombie dogs and lycans from *Underworld*. The carcass was seven to ten feet long and looked like it would burst if it were poked. I wondered if it was a victim of the rougarou or an unfortunate member of the species. It also crossed my mind that it was a mutant from the space testing area. No matter what it was, the entire boat was shocked.

The rest of the trip was peaceful. The icing on the cake was when we spotted two large boars at the end of a canal. They smelled horrendous but nowhere near the mysterious creature we'd encountered minutes earlier. The monster pigs trampled through the mud and were not happy we interrupted them. I wished them good luck because I knew the gators and Honey Island Swamp monster would be hunting them soon.

We made it back to the dock, and I was happy to get a picture with the captain. I hung out in the store and waited for everyone to head out, then approached him for some questions. He was happy to chop it up. He admitted that he really didn't know what that carcass was. It didn't look like other gator bodies, but that was the only known thing that is that big in the swamp. And when they swell up, they become unrecognizable. I agree with that.

He described a couple of after-dark encounters with unknown creatures. He has heard strange sounds and purrs coming from the trees that had a peaceful tone. Other nights, he has been forced out of fishing spots by intimidating roars and rocks being thrown in his direction. Tree knocks, whistles, and whispers were just a part of the swamp; he laughed.

Strange carcass.

He told me about another crazy experience that had happened a couple of years ago. He was fishing with his two friends deep in the swamp. There were three house-boats tied to each other, and they were fishing beside them. His friend got snagged under the house and caused a ruckus trying to get it undone. A man with an automatic .22 stumbled out of one of the doors.

The swamp man said that if there wasn't a fish on the end of the line; then he was going to shoot. They got the snag undone, and of course there was no fish. The crazy guy said, "Well, you heard me," and let off a barrage of shots. My captain ducked down and got the boat in motion. They escaped but were at a dead end. The guy knew and was waiting for them when they passed by. He let off more shots and hit the boat multiple times.

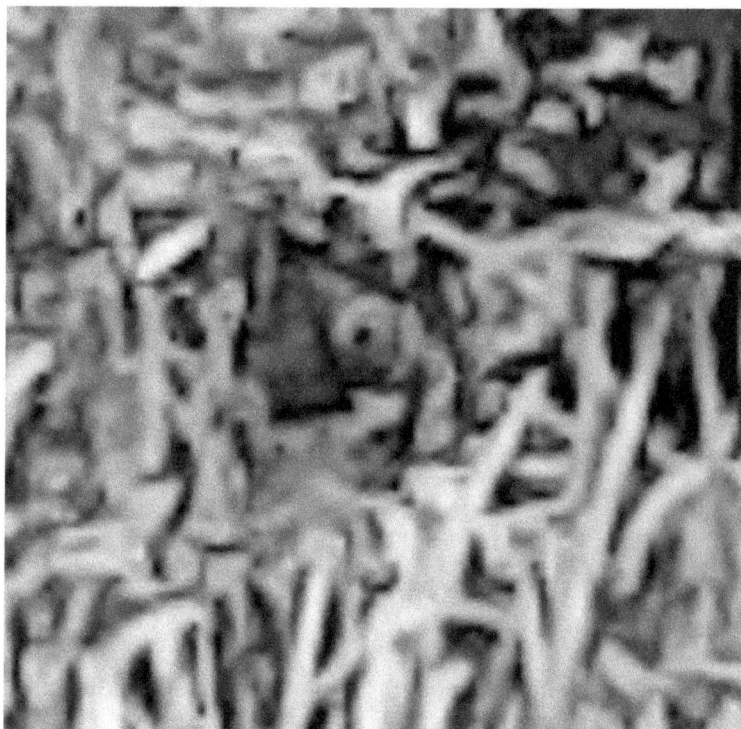

Dark face, big eye

They made it back to safety and reported it to the authorities. They sent out a sheriff, and the guy shot at him too. They surrounded his house with the entire force and had choppers ahead. Some old guy rowed up and asked if they were looking for his brother. He assured them he would bring him out if they promised not to hurt him. There was loud shooting within the unit, but the man surrendered and was apprehended.

The man's original charges of attempted murder on a police officer were reduced to simple assault. The man was back on the water within the week. He later put a shotgun in a cop's mouth and then was taken away for good. The man pleaded insanity and got locked in the looney bin.

The most interesting part was that he was a genius and used to work for the space program. He left for some odd reason and moved to the middle of the swamp. He was clearly very paranoid. Maybe he knows more about the origins of the Honey Island Swamp monster or whatever else they have hiding in that pristine land.

CHAPTER 11
DESOTO DEMONS
DESOTO NATIONAL FOREST, MISSISSIPPI

Cursed idol

T he Desoto National Forest is a serene getaway for trailblazers and fishermen, but when the sun goes down, it's probably smart to stay in your tent. People have been vanishing at a terrifying rate from our national parks and forests. There is a deeper reason for the land being protected by federal law. Many people of the bayous were carved by the giants. The battle of angels and demons might be going on right outside our tents.

Some believe that there are four types of people on this planet. Human, Sasquatch, red-haired giants and the grays. The zeta manipulated the bigfoot DNA about thirteen thousand years ago. Six thousand years ago, the population exploded, and now there are many species that roam the Earth. The pituitary gland in their brain regulates their height at a different rate than a human, and they can reach thirty feet tall. They have been working underground digging a labyrinth of caverns below our feet as we speak.

Teddy Roosevelt was one of the country's more respectable presidents. His book *The Wilderness Hunter* was about outdoor adventures and struggles in the mountain states. He describes a story of a trapper who was kidnapped and killed by a mountain beast. The partner of the deceased first relayed the story to Theodore, and the president was deeply moved. Another hunter had been killed and eaten at the same place the year before. Many prospectors and trappers have sadly met the same fate.

Even though many disappearances point in Sasquatch's direction, there are many positive experiences with this species. There are countless reports of young boys and girls playing with the children of the forest. Making mud pies, sharing fishing techniques, and even working together to hunt. Some kids realized their friend was different, but others treated the creatures just like any other pal.

Mother 'squatches have been known to look after vulnerable hikers. They can sense when humans are disabled or in need of help. A man claimed a female bigfoot shielded him and his handicapped son from an aggressive bear. There are many Native American legends that describe the troglodytes inheriting healing abilities and supernatural spirits.

Homo sapiens and Smy-a-likh have been sharing the land for thousands of years. The wild people are deeply connected to Mother Nature and her electric fields. This connection opens doors to heightened senses and abilities. The mitochondrial DNA of these creatures is female human while the nebular DNA is unknown male. This groundbreaking info opens the possibilities of Nephilim, watchers and fallen angels still roaming the forests today among man. Our connection to our creator might be closer than we understand. It is already written in our genetics; we just need to unlock the code.

Native American legends and proverbs speak a lot about the game keepers. They refer to them as stick Indians, tricksters, and frighteners. They are looked at as the evil god of the woods and a living solid force. The brushman and bushman's negative encounters are recounted as warnings and terrifying campfire tales. But some of the stone coats have protected and guided the First Nations people over the years, and it's interesting to wonder how they shaped our outdoor days of the present time.

Accounts of trading, hunting, and fishing together are not uncommon. Friendly masked beings and ottermen love to help their little brothers. The elder people would mimic animal calls and attract the prey, and the tribes would trap and kill the target. They would share the deer, pigs, and snakes while building bridges out of mud and leaves. There are many stories of the natives treating injured treemen and even more stories of the ancient beings using special abilities to perform miracles on us humans.

These ancient people have adapted perfectly to the natural world. They have sonar like dolphins and bats, infrasound like lions and tigers, and the ability to use their feet like monkeys do. Their vision is like an eagle mixed with a predator. They sense vibrations like alligators and can communicate with stomps from miles away like elephants.

Translucent hair allows the Sasquatch to camouflage to their surroundings. They are masters of disguise but have a problem masking one thing. Their smell is horrendous! The mixture of rotten skunk and dead fish pours into the surroundings and intoxicates the victims. The roadkill fragrance serves as a warning to most but a spell to others. You think a skunk's spray is bad, wait 'til you smell the skunk ape's. Their territory is marked.

Most adult male Sasquatch behaviors are to intimidate. A protective mother is even more dangerous. When the vibe is playful or curious, it is most likely a juvenile or young female. Their tree breaks and other markings are similar to our road maps. Most hikers walk right past without a second glance. But when a small number of us can read their signs, they begin to notice.

We slept outside a church right by the park perimeter. The boys set up the tent, and the girls said they would sleep in the car. Of course, when we were setting up our sleeping bags, they decided they were going to sleep in the tent as well. I had a bad headache, so I moved my stuff into the car. I'd much rather suffer alone.

I sipped some Gatorade and ripped the chillum. I tried to get my breathing right. Seven-seconds in and seven-seconds out. I massaged that sensitive pressure point between my thumb and index finger. Migraines make me delirious. There was a constant buzzing in the back of my head. I was sweating and probably had a fever. After a while, I lost track of time and finally passed out.

I was hiking a path that looked familiar with my mom and Pepa. I felt like I was back at the farm but could recognize some of the spots because I had just hit them earlier that day. We continued forward and for some reason my mom insisted that she separate from the pack. I was severely against it, but my grandfather didn't seem to care.

Next thing I know, my grandpa and I are trekking down a hillside toward a bank and a creek. A strange feeling overwhelmed me, and I knew something was wrong. Pepa stopped in his tracks, and I was already halted. I could feel that something was hiding behind one of the thicker trees. We creeped at an angle until we got a visual. Finally, I locked eyes on it.

The thing looked like a black-faced baboon. It looked like the thing was wearing a charcoal-colored Jabbawockeez mask. The creature's skin was ashy gray and badly burnt by the sun. The lurker was terrifying. I was paralyzed in my steps and just let out a loud shriek. That was my only defense; my body couldn't physically move. I felt the leer.

The creature was around the same height as me but could have been eighty years old. It is hard to put an age on something so obscure. The burnt skin and black eyes are what stood out to me. I just wanted to run towards my mom and make sure she was safe. Then there was a banging on the glass…

CHAPTER 12
PASCAGOULA PROWLER
MOSS POINT, MISSISSIPPI

The rougarou has been prowling and patrolling Pascagoula long before the Phantom Barber terrorized the region. Monster alligators, poisonous snakes and hogs the size of cars know to avoid the Werewolf of Fever Swamp. The local tribesmen have stories and encounters that date back to the beginning of the land while the people of the bayou are still encountering this beast to this day. Protect your pets along Pascagoula, the prowlers are closer than you think!

Entrance to the Prowlers lair

Creatures and mystery are no stranger to Mississippi. Ancient tribes once inhabited these lands and mysteriously vanished, leaving behind ruins and artifacts. There have been countless mounds and temples discovered throughout the state. They have excavated giant skeletons from those camps. Some believe bayous in the south were carved out by the giants that Jack slayed.

In 1973, the entire town of Pascagoula had UFO fever after hundreds of people witnessed unexplained lights in the sky. The Navy clocked a vehicle moving at incredible speeds over the bay. But two men encountered the otherworldly beings near a shipyard on an uncomfortable level. They were later picked up by police and relayed their story. While catfishing, they witnessed multiple creatures climb out of a spacecraft hovering above the water. The three aliens took the men after they fainted in terror.

The creatures took the guys to a brightly lit room on the ship. There was a giant floating eyeball that inspected and scanned them up and down. The beings had no eyes, pincer hands, and gray elephant skin. A feminine creature inspected them and put her fingers down their throat and nose. After choking, she telepathically told them everything would be okay.

The next thing the men knew, they were back on the fishing pier. The men were unharmed but terrified. One ditched his clothes because he was scared he would contaminate the world with his alien germs. The police recorded the men, and it's stunning. The story made national news and was one of the first alien abduction mysteries of modern America.

We started the morning off heading to the Gulf Coast Gator Ranch in Moss Point. I was stoked. I had seen the place on a couple of episodes of *Gator Boys*! On the drive, Adam and I played the audio from the alien abduction news cases. We knew there were beings in the sky, but we were worried about the violent rougarou and bigfoot encounters locals had reported.

Two boys were walking with their German shepherd in the woods. The dog ran off ahead and came back almost immediately whimpering. They continued farther and saw a freshly killed boar. The hind legs were snapped in two. The ribs of the pig were impaled on the nearby pine tree. The symbol must have been a warning or tribal marker.

We arrived at the gator ranch and signed up for an airboat tour. I admired all the cool knickknacks of the gift store and asked the lady at the front desk if she had seen any strange creatures around. She said the dinosaurs out back were strange enough. But she did say that they filmed the TV show *Killing Bigfoot* right around the region.

Before we knew it, our captain, Sam, was giving us the rules and regulations of the rougarou. That's right, our boat was named after the famed creature I was hoping to encounter. Adam's parents laughed but were probably embarrassed when I asked if we would see any on our tour. Sam replied that we just might and that his grandma used to warn him of the beast every time he left the house.

We tore the waterways up with the fan boat. Sam was drifting and splashing like Paul Walker in *Into the Blue*. He showed us a blind gator named Ray Charles. He sure was happy to see us. He had a collection of marshmallows in his marsh way. We pulled deep in the back of a lagoon, and he called for his gator friends. He gave off a loud coughing grunt and then called them like they were dogs.

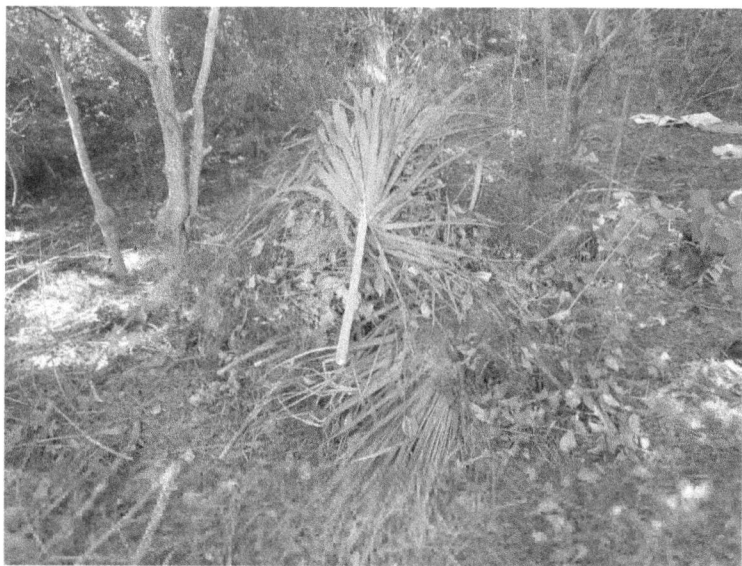

Shelter I discovered

In a few of the spots, the gators came right up to the boat, and in others there was no response. One narrow canal had a couple of baby alligators, so we began to search for the big bull. Sam said there is one big alpha for every 250 acres. We were determined to find it. He turned the fan down and just coasted down the narrow stream.

I shielded my face from the tree branches and kept my eyes out for snakes. We checked every crevice for the dinosaur. We spotted some slide marks and could smell that he was nearby, but he must have been dug up in the mud. We got to a part that was so thick, the only choice we had was to turn around.

Other side of the shelter

I had noticed a strange feeling but just attributed it to the monster gator. Now the feeling of dread was knocking on my door. I could sense something was near.

We had swum too far. I panned from left to right, searching for the source of this terror. The brush was thick, and there was near zero visibility, but I knew it had eyes on us. The horror felt like the sun but was subtle as well.

Sam noticed that I was scanning, and he worked his best to get that boat turned around. I think he had noticed it well before I did. We kicked off the trees but got her straightened out. He fired it up, but the motor started spitting. That was when the rest of the boat finally picked up on the unusual vibe coming from the swamp, but I had already been visualizing the Creature from the Black Lagoon for what felt like hours.

As the group stared at Sam, I nudged Adam, but he was already nose up like a dog. The pungent alligator smell had worsened into damp clothes, a chemically poisoned smell. It reeked like there was a den of roadkill buried away back in the hideout. The nest had to be nearby. There were bent trees and a still feeling in the air. I felt like we were surrounded, but luckily Sam got the boat running, and we jetted out of there.

When we slowed down, Sam said poachers were very common in the area, and he thought we might have spooked one of them. Adam and I smirked at each other, but the other families bought it. We found the big bull gator in a lagoon near a wooden bridge on the way back, and Adam saw a giant prehistoric alligator gar too. Never know what's going to happen out there.

We got a picture with the captain and walked the

ranch grounds. There were baby gators, eggs, and a boardwalk that took us over the water. There were dinosaurs everywhere. We saw a seventeen-foot bully that reminded me of Utan, the crocodile. I saw him in Myrtle Beach, and he's the largest held in captivity in the world. I imagined this place during a hurricane, and a chill went up my spine. It was time to go!

After the ranch, Adam and I were in the mood for some trails. We hit Shepard State Park and took off toward the tall trees along Pascagoula River and bayou. They were doing some construction on a cool river-walk pathway that journeyed over the swampland about twelve feet up from the ground. Some of the parts were incomplete, so we had to jump across from beam to beam.

It was risky because it was swampland in every direction, and there was no easy way back up or to safe land. There were gators, snakes and of course the prowlers lurking nearby. It was the fiftieth day of summer, the sun was shining, and the wind felt just right. I was having a blast and let off a couple of bigfoot roars. Immediately after, part of me regretted it because I didn't want to disrespect the natives of the land.

I had no problem balancing and jumping across the high beams. My biggest enemy was my own stomach. It was growling louder than the beast in the woods. On one of the larger gaps that we had to cross, I had to put a little bit of extra umph into it. And when I landed, my body just let go. I knew I had an emergency. There was a mess in my pants...

I waddled to the end of the river walk and turned around the way we came. I hopped across the same high beams that almost killed me with the gross wet underwear. I kept checking the back of my legs to make sure it wasn't running. It wasn't that bad, but it sure felt like a catastrophe. I wanted to keep my problem a secret.

After a mile in the compromised position, I could already feel the inside of my thighs near my pelvis were chafing. I was in pain. It was damn near bleeding; my skin was rubbed raw. Once we turned onto the path into the forest, I said I had to go to the restroom.

Adam continued going straight on the path, and I turned off to the left. I jogged out of sight and dropped my pants. As I was in my most vulnerable position, I almost shit myself again when I heard a loud ruckus just twenty yards from me in the thicket. I felt nauseous but knew I had to do something about my situation.

I stared off toward the sound and moved very slowly. I peeked down toward my underwear and saw that I had to get rid of them. I unraveled them from my cargo shorts and slipped my shoes off. I took my socks off and wiped myself the best I could. It was gross but needed to be done. I kept guard on the sound as I quietly buried my mistake.

I pulled my pants up and finally took a breath. I was hit with a rotten stench that almost knocked me over. I'm sure I was partially to blame for the foul odor, but I believe the creature released pheromones to warn me. It hadn't moved since the crash. The smell and feeling reminded me of a skunk or cat spraying but multiplied by ten. It was marking its territory and wanted me gone. I could sense that with every atom in me.

I put my shoes back on and ran toward Adam. He asked me if I had gotten lost, and I told him that I got a little turned around to just cover up my accident. I asked how long I was gone, and he said it was more than ten minutes. It only felt like thirty seconds to me.

We continued down the path, and I was just trying not to do any more damage to my legs. The prowler was in the back of my mind, but with each step feeling like I was being dragged across concrete, I had a more imminent threat. Though I was still confused about the time gap, I had to make sure to keep up with Adam. He rushed ahead and pointed toward a hole with a bunch of crab bones in it. It was cool but nothing groundbreaking.

We made it back to his parents and the campground in one piece. I went to the actual restroom and cleaned myself up as much as I could. I was thankful that I was able to manage it. I learned to always bring an extra pair of boxers with me! In the car, I pulled a tick out of my ear. Now that created a whole new level of paranoia. I will never forget the day the prowler made me poop!

CHAPTER 13
TEXAS WOOD BOOGERS
TYLER, TEXAS

The Cowboys and Redskins are one of the most heated rivalries in sports, but did you know they were on the same team? We all have heard that, "Everything is bigger in Texas" but also to "Beware of the boogeyman". Because before the Alamo, the cowboys and Indians were at war against the giants. Lines were drawn, and others were crossed, but still to this day the boogeyman lurks in the dark. Texas is filled with ghost towns, cartel horror stories and tales from the Wild, Wild West, but here's an explanation of why the Dallas Mavericks affiliate team is called the Texas Legends.

Even before the phantom of Texarkana caused towns to dread sundown, the boogeyman was lurking in the Longhorn State. The Fouke monster was making a buzz across the state line in Boggy Creek during the seventies.

The chupacabra lurks around the farms, and the dogmen patrol wildlands. After hours of driving across Texan plains, I felt like I was one of the leftovers heading to Jarden, searching for the sacred lands of Miracle, but I think that was just heat exhaustion. We needed to rest.

Me and Lyle Blackburn at the Great Florida Bigfoot
Conference. We were both featured speakers there.

A storm was approaching, and the sun was finally
going down, so we had to find somewhere to sleep

before we arrived in Dallas in the morning. We saw Tyler State Park ahead, and I thought that it would be a good idea to spend the night camping there. The other guys were not about it but knew we needed to pull over.

Tents and rain don't coincide in their book. They were both like witches scared to melt. Though, none of us were in the mood to deal with the ranger at the front desk, so I wasn't going to argue with them. We decided to just pull off on the side of the road and sleep in the Isuzu. Fine by me! I climbed in the trunk and listened to the rain.

After some exhausted peaceful minutes, I dozed off to sleep. The rain continued to pour, and I dreamt of my grandparents' farm. There was a dirt path that led to a magical pond. There were sharks that dug themselves in the mud and sand. I have visited that path many times in my dreams. As they approached the water, the leviathans rushed away and violently shook the ground. The vibrations woke me up.

Something had shaken the car. The storm was roaring, and the lightning completely illuminated the sky. The heavy rain felt like marbles being dropped on the aluminum. I slowly opened my eyes and wondered if there was a lightning bolt that had hit near the car. I just hoped it wasn't the police. There were no lights, and the other guys were still comatose. I peeked my eyes out the back and patiently waited for more lightning.

I scanned the wood line and down the road as far as I could see. I contemplated in my head if it was all in my dreams. If the heavy rain had just been playing tricks on my mind. I stared down the road again and looked for a hitchhiker. I know they like to mess with drivers or could have been just trying to get out of the rain.

I lay back down and tried to go back to sleep. My anxiety was running, and I had knots in my stomach. Usually I enjoyed the rain, but now my room (trunk) had begun to spin. I was nauseous and had to throw up. I opened the back door and puked right outside the car. The rain poured in, and the guys woke up.

I barely had anything in me but still felt like I was choking on whatever was in the back of my throat. I stuck my fingers down as far as I could reach and tried to empty out the toxins. The guys were drowsy but still laughing, telling me to get it all out. The stomach bile burned my insides as it poured from my mouth. I felt like I was blacking out and had a presence watching me.

I had the urge to slam the door shut but still had more to retch. I knew the smell would attract predators like chum in the ocean. I imagined the chupacabra latching onto my neck and sucking my blood as I was leaned over in a vulnerable position. I kept my watery eyes toward the darkness as I let out my last heave. I pictured Leatherface and his family surrounding our car.

I slammed the door shut and told the boys that we had to go. They just took it as I was sick and ready to get moving. But in my mind, impending doom was approaching. I felt like I had been attacked. The being had entered my dreams and turned my stomach upside down. I hadn't been drinking and didn't have food poisoning but was set in a trance state like I had been deep in both.

We took off toward Dallas, and I couldn't have been more relieved. I remained in the trunk and kept my eyes toward our parking spot. I tried not to blink as I searched the shadows for the perpetrator. I'm not sure if it was clarity or pareidolia, but I saw at least five sets of eyes closing in on where we just were. This was an organized onslaught.

We had a few hours until we could meet up with our couchsurfing host, so we stopped for breakfast. As we pulled into the diner, I was happy to get my feet on the ground. I went straight to the bathroom and wiped some clean water on my face. I looked into the mirror and saw my eyes were dilated. I looked like I was on drugs. My body was deeply affected. This wasn't just a fluke. My spirit was under fire.

The mixture of heat exhaustion and lack of sleep surely would have some powerful side effects, but it just didn't make sense. The terror was too vivid. I was already sleeping, and that was what my body needed most. Naturally, I didn't think my insides would do the opposite of what was helping. My body was in defense mode. Against an enemy that was previously unknown.

The guys made jokes during breakfast, but I was just focused on replenishing. I sipped my orange juice slowly and nibbled at my eggs and toast. I felt better but still had a blanket of strange feelings hovering over me. After we finished eating, we got a hold of our host and planned to meet in Dealey Plaza. As we approached the car, Bass noticed a few new dents and scratches. They blamed it on hail, but I knew exactly what it was... the boogeyman.

CHAPTER 14
DESERT APES
LAS CRUCES, NEW MEXICO

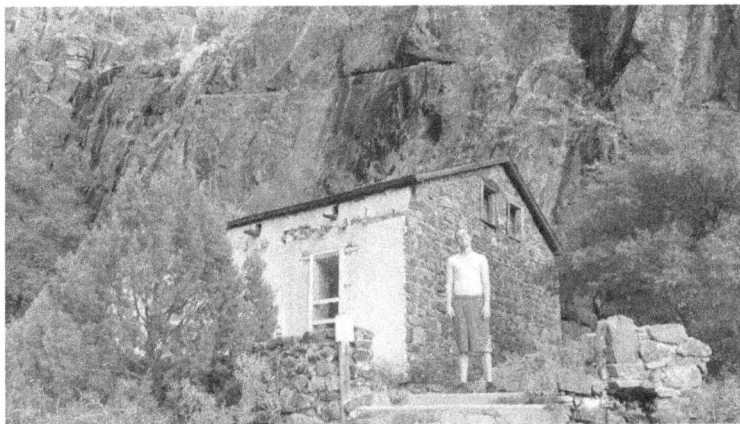

Old ruins in Las Cruces, New Mexico

Many native tribes believe we live on a giant turtle, and their beliefs have more roots in reality than what modern science teaches. We are surrounded by mud fossils. The golden-aged titans were turned to stone when the floods poured from the heavens, ending the Silicon Era. The Stone Age, Carbon Era began, and the remnants of the originals now stand as mountains. They are named the Organ Mountains for a reason!

The desert can play tricks on one's mind, but that still doesn't change the fact that the hills have eyes. In these very mountains there have been sightings of monsters and creatures since the beginning of time. UFOs roam the skies, and the chupacabra keeps the farmers up at night, but deep in the red rock, campers have been terrorized by tailless monkeys and desert apes with red eyes. Said to be a lost tribe of Natives, these giant clans of predators still call the sacred stone of Las Cruces and El Paso home.

Mexican favelas were to my left and the beautiful UTEP campus on my right when I arrived in El Paso. We survived a flood, an attempted carjacking, and a couple of ghost towns. And that was just between here and Dallas. That ten-hour drive felt like days in that Texas heat. It was cool to see the mountains the farther west we went, but we all know what that means, more mystery.

We pulled off to Dripping Springs in Las Cruces for a hike into the mountains. I was excited to get off the road for a bit and smoke a couple of joints in the red rock. We hit the visitors center and checked the map for our journey. I noticed a spot on the opposite side of the trail called Hermit's Cave. We needed to check that out.

The cave had been used for shelter by humans for five thousand years but was named after one of its 1800s residents. There was a medicine man named Giovanni Maria de Agostini. He traveled through Peru, Brazil, Chile and many other South and Central American countries. He walked across America and lived in Vegas for a while. He was sixty-two when he moved into La Cueva.

The monk healed people with herbs and potions and gained many followers. He lit a torch at the cave entrance every Friday evening to communicate with the outside world. Sadly, the fire went out when he was mysteriously murdered. Stabbed in the back with no leads. His murder was never solved. He is honored worldwide in festivals and parades, and his pilgrimage route is protected by the national park.

After paying our respects at the cave, we stopped for a water break before hitting the red path. I was excited to cool off in the springs and get an eye on this waterfall. I had climbed Dunn's River Falls in Jamaica, been on *Maid of the Mist* in Niagara, and explored countless Ohio cascades. It was time to add a more obscure visit to my collection.

The trail was more difficult than it appeared to be. There was a gradual incline that you could only feel in your legs. We passed many people on the way back, and they were all smiling. We were exhausted and wondering how these people found the energy. That spring really must have been like the fountain of youth.

Some hikers warned us that they'd seen a rattlesnake just ahead on the trail. We were on high alert; a bite this far from the parking lot and hospital most likely would be deadly. Each step was prepared with precaution. We continued forward with one eye on the mountains and the other on the trail. I jumped when I saw a giant tarantula but wanted it as a pet after a few minutes.

After some more hiking, we reached Boyd's sanitarium! We explored the ruins and searched for hidden mysteries. There used to be a hotel and resort up in the mountains that used the springs' healing characteristics to their advantage. I sat on the old porch and imagined the breath of life that used to pump through the valley. It was the closest to heaven that I had ever been.

We split up on the rest of the hike toward the springs. The trail broke off into multiple branches, and I took the high ground. I was exploring the large rock areas, searching for caves and hieroglyphs. Bass appeared on a ledge that looked impossible to reach, and Polk remained close to the main path, petrified of the heights.

The water was flowing, and the creek below was glistening. I climbed over to the water and took off my shoes. I swam in the knee-deep water, searching for little fish and fossils. I made cups with my hands and enjoyed the cold drink. I filled up our bottles and felt like a new man.

I was tying my wet hair in a ponytail when I felt like I was being watched. I checked for more hikers and searched all the locations we'd just entered, but saw no clues. The sun was going down soon, and the park would be closed, so I figured we were the last hikers on the dirt.

I kept my composure and continued searching crevices and hollows for anything I could find. But now in the back of my head, I wasn't looking for snakes and rabbits, I was on alert for mountain lions and black bears. I wasn't too nervous about the bobcats and coyotes, though a pack of them would be a problem. This presence was unlike anything natural in the forest that I have encountered. My sixth sense was ringing.

Sleeping Giant mudfossil

I made my way to Bass, and before I could even say anything, he told me we were being hunted. He thought he saw some movement in the distance. He believed tribes of people still inhabited the region and they terrorize anyone who stays too long. He was describing *The Hills Have Eyes*, but I had an idea of what might have been after us. I had heard many stories of the wild people who inhabited the red rock.

Giant's face

We got packed up and started back towards the car. The walk back was mostly downhill, but the sun was moving away quickly. We were in a race against the dark. I felt like I was on the run from vampires. We decided not to tell Polk. He was driving, and we needed his mind clear. Bass and I kept an eye on our six the entire time. We both felt we were still being pursued. We could feel a presence closing in on us.

The car was in sight, and the moon was creeping out. We were basically at the edge of the Earth, and the shadows were trying to swallow us. We kept our pace forward and luckily got back to the parking lot. We hopped in the car and slammed the doors behind us. I took a few deep breaths and sank deep into the seat. My spirit was exhausted, and my aura had been targeted. I felt like I was hiding from graboids and ducking monsters. I wouldn't have been surprised if we began to be hunted by the killer tire from *Rubber* at this point. The desert is a strange place! It consumes you!

CHAPTER 15
MOGOLLON MONSTER
FLAGSTAFF, ARIZONA

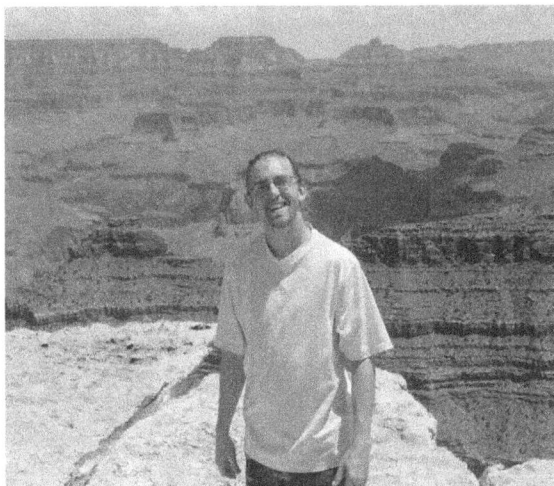

Search for Grand Canyon giants

The Grand Canyon is the fingerprint of our creator, an antenna for our universe to others like it. There is no wonder why the First Nations people gravitated to this magical wonderland of red rock. There have been many fascinating discoveries of bones, pottery, and artwork that give us some tangible evidence of some of the legends of skinwalkers, cavemen, and paranormal anomalies that have occurred in the canyon. Mysterious stories pile up daily, but the truth might just be under some rock layers or right up in the sky. Beware of Momo, the Mogollon Monster, the King of the Troglodytes.

The snapshot of the Grand Canyon cryptids appeared in my brain. I remembered seeing the three sets of eyes staring back at the camera flash from deep in the cavern. The silhouettes of the ferocious beasts took shape in my anxious mind. The helpless feeling of being surrounded was crawling in my skin.

On the long drive from California to Florida, we of course had to see the Grand Canyon. Heading toward Flagstaff, we drove through the Coconino National Forest. I had heard many mysterious stories out of Arizona. I knew the state led the nation in missing person cases and of course had talked to locals about the Phoenix Lights incident. Legends refer to eight-foot-tall hairy giants, tiny gray humanoid aliens, and portals to other worlds and dimensions. The Lakota locals call the Sasquatch *chiye* and *tanka*, meaning elder brother and great. Others refer to them as boor, brutes, and boobs.

There have been many disappearances over time at the Grand Canyon. We researched a few on the long drive. One tragic case was that of Morgan Heimer. He was a twenty-two-year-old white-water rafting guide.

He was a fit outdoorsman and more than capable of the work he was doing. He was on an eight-day rafting trip but sadly vanished on the sixth afternoon far down the river. He was separated from the group while walking back to camp after a day of rafting and was never seen again. The area was enclosed by cliffs, and he should have been found. No trace has ever been found of Morgan.

I also remembered personally following the search for Drake Kramer. He was just twenty-one and went missing after visiting the Grand Canyon. He sent some alarming texts to his family, so they reported him missing, but his body was never discovered. I always wondered how the cadaver dogs never found him. He was from the same neighborhood as a couple of people I met in the Lakeland area.

In 2016, just a year before we adventured through the canyon, a Tampa local went missing camping the big ditch. Floyd E. Roberts III was a former NASA employee, schoolteacher, and avid outdoorsman. He was on a nine-day hike with his best friend and his daughter. Floyd took a different route back to camp and sadly vanished on the very first evening. They called the search off after six days, and a tree was planted in Mr. Roberts honor.

Many different humanoid creatures have been spotted and discussed in myths and legends of the red rock rim. There are geoglyphs and hieroglyphs that depict an interesting history of the canyon. Some of the glyphs were even created by these mysteries themselves.

Caverns and underground facilities are rumored to exist where descendants of the originals still lurk. And when the sun goes down, they come out to worship the moon.

We stopped at a gas station and explored their tribal knickknacks. We filled up our gas tank and asked the worker where the best place to camp was. She told us about an RV park, but we were trying to save some money and go off grid. A person appeared from the back and told us about a perfect location a couple of miles from the street. Bass got the info, and we thanked both of them before disappearing into the night.

As we drove slowly, searching for the road to pull off to set up our tent, we joked about how creepy the gas station was. Polk joked that someone was definitely killed there. Dom remembered hearing a story he'd heard while couchsurfing in Tucson. A friend of his had been house-sitting and taking care of a family's animals. After a few strange nights of the goats freaking out, he had an encounter that changed his life forever. He walked in on a reptilian creature battling a werewolf for a goat that had its throat ripped out. On that note, we sparked a blunt and opened up a bottle of whiskey.

Luckily Dom spotted the road, and we found our spot for the night. We set up the tent and started singing songs in the wind. We were screaming at the top of our lungs, enjoying the freedom. I still remember our angsty folk songs! The entire trip had been so tiring and exhausting on our bodies. It felt really good to truly let loose. All those hours cooped up in the car had my joints and bones just begging to be shook out. So that was what we did.

We danced around the desert, acting like animals. We howled at the moon, barked like dogs, and called to the skies. The drinks kept pouring, and the ganja was burning. I stumbled over and got a bad cut on my knee. I laughed and wiped the blood on my face like tribal paint. The other guys thought it was brilliant and took turns slicing their fingers with their knives.

We settled down and formed a circle. We thanked each other for the companionship along this cross-country journey and each chose one of our items to bury. I threw my shark tooth in with a guitar pick, a hand-wrapped gem, and an old key. We each threw some dirt on top until it was fully covered. It was a special moment.

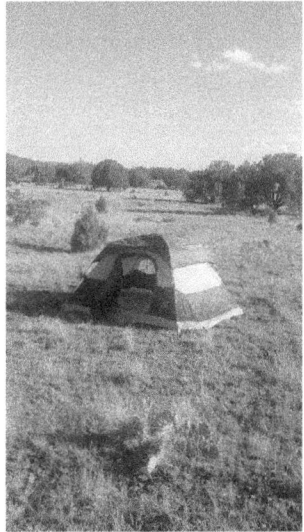

Primitive camping

Before we went to bed, we decided to do a quick group meditation. Back home at the Biltmore, the punk house in Lakeland, we partook in rituals and experiment daily. We do a multistep warm-up exercise and follow it with a deep meditation. We would do facial stretches, hum in harmony, shoulders to ears, mindlessly chatter, do leg and neck stretches and other things to warm our minds and bodies to enter a trance. We also used different crystals, incense, candles, and mists to induce a deeper state of dreamworld.

Next-level work included loud screams, curling up into a ball as tight as we could, and holding our breath. We would switch up invoking and lesser banning rituals and try new places like the backyard, near the lakes, and midnight at a cemetery. Over time we developed strong cohesion and invited others to join our meditations. The group aspect was a multiplier for vibrations. We inherited each other's skills and thrills, similar to the concept of *Sense8*.

We worshipped to the east at sunrise to Ra, south at noon to Hathoor, west at sunset to Tum and north at midnight to Khephera. We explored opposites like safety and danger, victory and defeat, pleasure and pain, good and evil, heaven and hell, god and the devil and of course love and death. For about me flames the pentagram, and in the column stands the six-rated star. We studied chakras, the stars, and many gods from the past.

We kept daily journals on the experiments and worked them into our artwork. We broke glass and dishes in the kitchen to relieve stress and push the boundaries. We made clothing, songs, and jewelry at all hours of the night that connected to our pinnacle project, the musical. We were family, and everything happened for a reason. It all had brought me to that point, deep in meditation in the middle of the Arizona desert.

Three of us climbed in the tent while our buddy from

LA chose to sleep in the car. The ground was hard and not level, but I was happy to be able to stretch my legs. I was in the middle and was the only one without a sleeping bag. We had a light on while we got situated. I was exhausted and dozing off when I was suddenly awakened by a scream.

I rolled over as my buddy was jumping out of his sleeping bag. He was yelling "Spiders! Spiders! It's covered in spiders!" My first instinct was to scoot away, but when I looked toward his sleeping bag, it looked normal. He was hallucinating. He was freaked out. I could see it on his face. I was scared too but luckily fell back asleep.

Hours later, I was awoken again when I heard something walking outside the tent. Before I opened my eyes, I guessed it was just one of the guys going to the restroom. But they were both still sleeping next to me, and I figured I would have heard the car door open and close. The sounds stopped, but I couldn't fall back asleep, and now I had to go to the restroom.

I pulled the zipper and crept out of the tent. I scanned the surrounding area and couldn't see a thing. There were cacti and bushes in every direction. I was fine peeing in the open, but I could only imagine what was lurking in the shadows. As I released, the wind picked up and there was a constant hum in the air. It was soothing but made the hair on the back on my neck stand up.

I sprayed back toward the camp, and as I reached

toward the entrance, I heard rustling in multiple locations. Whatever made the sound did so with intention
and clearly had eyes on me. I crawled over my buddy,
under my blanket and dug my head into my backpack
pillow. I wished for morning.

The sounds continued and closed in toward the tent. I
did not feel threatened. I felt that the creatures were just
curious because they were not used to seeing people
spend the night out here. The strong smell of my dehy-
drated urine may have intrigued them too. I was nervous
the creatures thought that I was marking my territory.

Luckily I ended up falling asleep and was woken up
in the morning by the car door slamming. The guys were
out of the tent, and our west coast rider was nowhere to
be found. We searched the area and screamed his name
but had no luck. His phone was still in the SUV, so we
were a little worried. We had no choice but to pack up
and just wait. I searched for animal tracks or any clues.

We drew up multiple plans and penciled in even
more theories. We smoked what we had left just in case
we would have to call the police. We debated even
calling the police. We wondered if he just went on a
morning walk or maybe got picked up by a trucker. I was
worried he got bit by a rattlesnake and was just outside
of yelling range. I imagined him suffering, and it hurt me
bad. We screamed his name some more.

I walked off in the opposite direction of the road. I
scoured the area, searching for pieces of clothing, parts of
his belongings, or sadly even one of his dreadlocks. The

creeping sounds of the previous night lurked in my mind. I wondered if the sounds had been him. I was mad at myself for not going out earlier. Or even just checking the car when I got done peeing. But I had been scared myself!

I stared at the mountainside and imagined the possibilities. He could be anywhere out there. Anything could be out there. Maybe it was a mountain lion… or a pack of javelinas. The collared peccaries sure are mean. Maybe it was bigfoot that got him, or did the aliens beam him up? I really didn't know. I was lost in a daze. I missed sleeping in beds. I missed my mom.

I lost track of time and lost sight of the car. I wandered in the opposite direction of the mountains and finally reached the road. I followed the white line for a while and finally saw my gang waving their arms. I picked up the pace when I saw it was three of them. I was ecstatic that LA had made it back safely. I ran toward them, and they all seemed so worried.

They embraced me with hugs and asked me where I was. I told them I was searching for LA and got a little turned around. Polk and Bass asked, "For five hours?" I laughed, puzzled. "Maybe fifty minutes." And then pointed to LA's chest. "Where were you?" And I could tell by his body language that he was confused. He dribbled, saying he woke up outside the gas station where we first stopped. We were all speechless but hopped back on the road for the next adventure.

CHAPTER 16
MOJAVE SANDMAN
MOJAVE DESERT, CALIFORNIA

Labyrinth below

The desert is full of mirage, mystery, and monsters, and the Mojave has its fair share of mayhem. If you can survive the heat in Death Valley, beware of the rattlesnakes, mountain lions, and canyon cannibals. A long list of missing persons, countless UFO sightings and legends of portals keep even the most experienced outdoorsman on their toes. When visiting the Mojave, pack some extra water and make sure to respect the land of the Sandman.

The Mojave is a magnet for strange occurrences. Satanic cults, violent murders, and legends of lost treasure are flooding the dunes. There are stories of walking cactus and boulders that swallow people who sleep on them. There are mysterious patches of grass that grow exotic mushrooms in the middle of the desert. People believe they are fairy portals because they are there one minute and gone the next. The land is unexplainable.

Many people have claimed to have seen spaceships in the Mojave. Others claim to have been abducted straight from the red rock. Bigfoot and gnomes have been spotted emerging from these craft. Hundreds of people witnessed an unknown aircraft crash in the forest in Barstow. The men in black covered it all up. There are rumors of underground government bases and alien cities underneath the San Andreas fault and Hoover Dam. How many mirages until it's accepted as reality?

There have been many bones of prehistoric Indians found in the desert. Jawbones five times the size of an average man have been discovered. In the early settler days, the skeleton of Satan himself was on tour in the west. The legend of the Lovelock giants is still told around campfires up to this day. The old owner of the museum used to display some of the bones. I called the other day, and they claimed the bones never existed... but I have seen the pictures!

In the early 1900s, prospectors found tracks of a giant animal. There were legends of giant lizards and troglodytes that roamed the land, so the find had the region roaring. The experienced trackers were confused by the size of the footprint. The shape was not reptilian and not humanlike. The print looked like it came from the Ice Age. It resembled a mammoth elephant foot. I imagine a Regirock.

Locals were puzzled. Still to this day, it is debated if the behemoth species had survived over ten thousand years in American caves or if one flew from Africa like the cartoon "Dumbo". Others were quick to call it a hoax. But word got out that a traveling circus had abandoned an elderly elephant while passing through. This story wrapped things up for some, but many still believe that giants still roam the desert.

There are many caves and abandoned mine shafts in the region. These deep dwellings could be the perfect home to predators and these mysterious monsters. Others believe they could be entrances to middle earth, alien ships, and government bases. Near Area 51, Kenny Veach found a cave in the shape of an M. While approaching the cave, his body was overrun by strong vibrations. Weeks later he disappeared trying to explore the area further. He has still never been found.

I crushed up Hawaiian baby wood rose seeds and put them in a shot glass of water. I filtered the seeds and left it overnight. It created a tea that I drank the next morning. Ancient tribes used to do this, seeking enlightenment. I got a really bad stomachache and began to vomit. I lay on the rocks and tried to grasp reality. The tincture has many levels of effects. Sometimes a body buzzes and other times, full-on oblivion. This time was inversion.

I was hiking the red rock and had a bunch of gear on my back. I saw a camp up ahead, so I approached slowly, looking for another hiker. Out of the tent climbed a person whom I recognized, but I couldn't place who it was. I yelled out and expected him to turn around, but he couldn't hear me. I moved towards him, still calling out and trying to flag him down. I got within ten yards of him, and he had to hear me by now.

It was the MMA fighter who went missing out here. When that clicked, we both turned our heads toward a crash that sounded like an earthquake about two hundred yards away. We both took off in the opposite direction with no hesitation. He led the way as I ducked and dodged bushes and holes. We made it to an overhang and each took positions keeping guard in opposite directions. I fell asleep, and he was gone when I woke up.

I was with my dad and sister on a tour of Lake Mead and the Hoover Dam. We took a bus from Vegas through the treacherous desert. The guide explained many mirages and Death Valley legends. He spoke of the most deadly lake in America, Area 52 below the dam, and the mutant that roamed the Mojave. He said we would pass Denzel Washington's and Michael Jordan's homes.

We pulled off to see some bighorn rams at a park. It was stunning watching them crash into each other. The sound was so loud. I felt it in my chest. Luckily my stomachache was gone. I knew I was twenty-one again, and it was my birthday. The short hair felt great in the breeze. I stared off into the canyon, and the mountains began to move. They shredded their stone and showed their colors. All new to my eyes. They battled with swords and spears. Two imitated the rams below and crashed right towards me.

I woke up, and I was in the car with the Suicide Boys blaring. The boys shook me awake and said that we were almost to LA. I was twenty-four and homesick. I was delirious from the endless nights on the road and half sleep, but the smell of Hollywood woke me up like the spirit of hartshorn. I stared out the window as Bass played an episode of *Death Valley* on his phone. More zombies, vampires, and mutants. I needed a Hawaiian shot; it had been too long.

After some bigfoot badder, I was in my backyard in Lakeland, picking oranges from the tree. I heard yelling coming from inside the house. Midway through a Dungeons & Dragons quest, my guild was trapped inside an evil monster's lair. I located the stream in the valley and followed it all the way up the mountain. I shared my food with a coyote, and he followed me up. We came upon a cave, and I heard screams from inside.

I ran towards the noise and saw flames illuminating the Sandman's den. There were beautiful paintings and carvings blanketing the walls. I heard my friends calling and saw a large shadow up ahead. I shot my slingshot and hit it in the back of the head. I drew my knife and ran right towards it. I leaped and aimed for the neck. The beast turned around and swiped me hard into the wall. It prowled after me, but the coyote jumped and knocked it off balance. The ceiling crashed down, and I ran towards my clan's voices while the dust blinded me. The Yucca man still haunts me.

CHAPTER 17

BIG BEAR BEAST

SAN BERNARDINO COUNTY, CALIFORNIA

Sketch of the Beast

Big Bear is an oasis near the middle of Sin City and the City of Angels. These mountains are famous for their skiing, biking, and of course big ol' bear. The high altitude provides a unique environment for the ecosystem to thrive. Floyd Mayweather and Mike Tyson have trained in the magic mountains before championship fights, but I can guarantee to you that they were not the most dangerous thing in those forests.

Sasquatch sightings are very popular in Big Bear. They were extremely prominent in the later months. The beasts lurk around like Snover in their winter coats, terrorizing snow skiers and people riding snowmobiles. The Abomasnow monsters use the caves and cliffs in the region for shelter and cover from the weather.

California is no stranger to Sasquatch sightings. Bluff Creek is the Garden of Eden in the bigfoot world. I was lucky enough to be a guest on the Bluff Creek podcast roundtable. I chopped it up with many people who have camped at the location of the famous Patterson-Gimlin footage. I even had the pleasure of being friendly roasted by Carl Crew, the nephew of Jerry Crew, the man who originally found the footprints with his construction crew. I will physically camp at Bluff Creek one day; remote viewing only takes me so far.

For my twenty-first birthday, my dad treated my sister and me to a vacation in the mountains of Big Bear Lake. His childhood friend owned a cabin in the heart of the basin and was happy to let us visit. We flew into Las Vegas and made the four-hour drive to the mountains after a couple of days of golden nights.

We rented a PT Cruiser and almost didn't make it. We survived the UFO hotbed in Barstow, but the rest of the path was treacherous. There was a very bad rainstorm, and we had to cross a flooded road with raging water. There was a huge cliff, and we were ready to ditch the car if it got stuck. Huge boulders and debris were moving at fast speeds. We didn't have much choice because we were already deep in the valley, and there was only one road. Plus we were sure the road had been washed out behind us. Luckily we survived.

The cabin was amazing. They had a basketball hoop, a patio with an amazing view and a lot of cool memorabilia from the region. They had pottery, fossils, jewelry and mystical paintings. There was a shed in the back with a guest room above it. Within an hour of being there, I was plotting out how to move in. I was snooping in the garage and found some fishing poles, the four-wheelers, and one thing that caught my eye. A plaster bigfoot print!

We went into town to explore and to get groceries. We stopped at some shops and stands. I saw many different stone statues of bigfoot and large bears. That plaster cast was still on my mind. There were totem poles and impressive woodwork in every direction. We picked up the essentials and headed back to the cabin.

My sister was outside having a cigarette; the neighbors noticed some new faces and invited her back for a drink. I went with my sister while my dad made dinner. The guys were cool. They were gold prospectors, born and raised in the San Bernardino Valley. They said Bear Mountain used to be called Goldmine Mountain. He had a small container of gold that he had found. Small pieces were really heavy.

He offered up a joint, and I cracked open another beer. He was telling us stories of why he had to carry protection while prospecting. He said that he had almost been robbed on multiple occasions. He kept saying it was the Wild, Wild West out there, and some gold mines had not been explored in a hundred years; you just had to find them. While we were in his garage, looking at his collection of guns, we heard a loud animal noise off in the distance. He laughed and said, "That's another reason!" It could have been a bear, wolf, or even domesticated dog.

But I asked, "Bigfoot?" and he asked how I knew. I told him I'd found a plaster cast at the cabin and that I'd had other encounters with the species back home. He smiled and pulled out two big but different casts of his own. One only had four toes. He said he'd seen the four-toed one less than a mile from there and that he was very aggressive. He said that was probably him that roared. He liked the swamp right off the trail.

My dad called, and it was time for dinner. We thanked them for their hospitality, and they gave us a handful of their homegrown. It was a nice gesture and made the mountains even more magic. Only thing equivalent to gold. As I dapped him up, he warned me to never go into the woods after dark. I thanked him and ran off.

The next morning we ate at the Grizzly Cafe and had

plans to go zip-lining. The cafe was awesome. A perfect small-town spot with great food and even better service. I asked our waitress if any professional boxers had come through, and she said there had been many celebrities who passed by. I then asked her if anyone had mentioned seeing bigfoot, and she chuckled and said quite a few people. Even her grandson, on her property! I elbowed my dad and had a burst of energy. We finished breakfast, thanked her with a tip and were off.

Bird's eye view, zip lining in Big Bear

We were having a great time. Laughter is the best loving. We rode through the beautified curvy roads while I kept thinking of boxers, bigfoot and the Dorner cabin, the place they burned the rogue cop alive after he killed multiple people and led one of the biggest manhunts in modern history. We eventually arrived at the Action zip-lining place, and I couldn't be more pumped.

We filled out the paperwork in case we fell to our death and then immediately were off with our group. We hopped in Swiss Army trucks and went on an hour mile trek up the side of the mountain. They told us that we would have great views of Johnson Valley and the highest peak in SoCal, Mount San Gorgonio. I was intoxicated with outdoor vibrations. This was sacred land. Pristine grounds for mowgli wickiups.

We flew from treetop to treetop. It was pure serenity when we were on the zip line. I peered between the trees, searching for deer, ram, and of course our wookie friends. The scariest part was when we reached the end of the cable and had to strap into the tower. The beams shook, and I was terrified of the entire thing collapsing. My knees shook, and my balls were in my stomach.

On one of the last runs, I had trouble slowing down and crashed into the metal beam. The worker tried to slow down the collision, but it was inevitable. Luckily my head was safe, but my legs got scraped up pretty bad. The staff sent me down the last zip line ahead of the group so I could receive medical attention.

I followed our driver to the truck, and he was going to patch me up. I asked him if anyone had ever gotten seriously injured here. He said just some scrapes and bruises for visitors. But workers had had broken bones after hours, not using the right safety precautions. He mentioned that they had had some other scares too. I asked him what he meant as we finally got eyes on the truck. He was just about to answer me as we heard rustling behind the vehicles.

We approached slowly, and the staff member took the lead. I figured it was just another guide who was getting something out of the trunk, but clearly the worker knew something was up. His coworkers were still on the zip lines, and the rest were at the bottom of the mountain. As we crept through the rocks and turned the corner of the trucks, the sound was gone.

The staff grabbed the first aid kit and walked me back towards the group. He poured peroxide on my knee and pulled out some bandage wrap. I could see that his hands were shaking really bad. I asked him what he thought it was. He quickly uttered, "A bear. It was a bear." I knew he wasn't being completely honest.

Moments later, my sister and dad came marching down the hill with smiles on their faces. I was confused but still having a great time. The crash and cuts were just part of the outdoor adventure. I was just glad the cable didn't snap and I didn't break my neck. My injuries would heal, but the empty void on that hillside grew in my mind.

The next day we took the ski lift to the Summit Resort. The moving chair was scarier than the Millennium Force and Top Thrill Dragster combined! At least in the winter, the snow gives you a false sense of security. If you fall in the fluffy snow, you have a chance of survival.

It was the end of summer, and down below was just dirt. I searched for animals and watched the downhill bikers to keep my mind off the heights.

The view from the mountaintop was worth the fright I felt. The food was incredible, and the air was clean. We sat next to a group of guys who rented a cabin there every summer. They told us about delicious restaurants and a wood carver to check out. They told me that I must hit the lake since I was a fisherman. I told them it was on my list.

I asked them if they'd heard of any bigfoot activity in the area while they had been visiting. They looked at each other, and one spoke up. He said that from time to time, they would hear knocking on the side of their cabin in the middle of the night. And whenever they went out to investigate, there was no sign of the perp. They had seen bent trees and dead animals on the property but nothing too out of the ordinary.

When we got back to our cabin, I was inspired by the bikers and in X-Games mode. My dad had multiple ATVs in the garage, and I was set on blazing the trails. We checked the four-wheelers, and sadly only one was operable. We decided to take turns, and my dad went first. He was gone for ten minutes and came back with a grin from ear to ear.

I took the quad out next. I ripped the dirt trail like Travis Pastrana and Kenny Bartram. I was a cowboy now! I squinted my eyes as the wind kissed my cheeks. I lost track of time and wasn't sure how much juice this ride had. I did a 180 and noticed a figure paralleling me from my right side. I knew it wasn't a person, but it was moving too fast to ID it.

I remembered the footprint cast from the prospector. Something with feet that size would have a stride large enough to easily keep up with my mini ATV. I pulled the lever with my right hand and gunned the four-wheeler as fast as it could go. I wasn't sure if the creature continued to follow me, but I was not taking any risks. I peeled into the driveway, and my dad threw his arms up.

I told him something was out there and that Erin shouldn't go. He could tell that I was actually in fear and took the quad right into the garage. I wondered if he'd encountered the same thing while he was out riding. He was more afraid of bears and mountain lions than all the creatures I feared.

Moments later, my sister came outside, all ready to ride. Her mood changed when she saw that it was back packed away. She threw a fit, but we said it was getting too dark. I feel bad that she never got to ride, but it may have saved her life. Sadly, my dad's friend sold the cabin, but one day I hope to return to the mountain.

CHAPTER 18
ACROSS THE WORLD

Gopher Gang

There have been reports of the wildman since the beginning of time on all continents of the world. North America is the home of Sasquatch, Australia has the yowie, and the yeren calls Asia home. The yeti and abomination snowman patrol the cold regions while the skunk ape and rock apes patrol the swamps and jungles. The truth of their existence has been proven; now it's time to figure out who they are.

The North American bigfoot has been spotted from the icy shores of British Columbia to the sunny beaches near the Everglades. Native Americans and First Nations people learn from a young age to respect our forest elders. They have been taught not to go into the forest after dark and, if they do encounter the creatures, to proceed with extreme caution. The indigenous people traded, coincided, and sadly battled the tribe of lost giants. But the bond is still strong, and that may be the reason that the species feel more comfortable on reservation land.

Down under, the Aussies named their creature the yowie. They also refer to it as the yaroma, wawee, jimbra and tjangara. The aboriginals know of two different species of these beasts on their island. One stands tall like the American Sasquatch, and the other is between four to five feet tall. Ancient cave art depicts these two cryptids walking side by side. Sightings are popular on the east side of the continent. The Pilliga Scrub is a hot spot. Many people avoid driving through after dark. The joonjari have been known to feast on kangaroos and are fearless of humans. In the Yarra Ranges, yowies are known to keep Melanesian leopards as pets and hunting companions.

Patagonia literally means land of the giants. Spanish explorers encountered a twelve-foot, two-headed giant while surveying new lands. They battled, and it killed four of the pirates. The men finally slayed the titan with a spear to the heart. They mummified the creature and later toured it with a circus. It has been tested and has been ruled authentic. There is a lot of ancient English lore about giants and behemoths.

Makeshift camp

In Shennongjia, there is a statue of a mother Yeren embracing her child. It is a popular spot for tourists to snap a photo. In the land of giant pandas, clouded leopards and golden snub-nosed monkeys, this elusive creature is looked at as a protector. The existence of the Yeren is common knowledge, and ancient texts show that humans and these creatures have done more than just live on the same mountainside.

In the mid-1800s, there was a Neanderthal ape lady named Zana captured in Russia. They broke her will over time and used her as a slave. She had multiple children with men of the village. The first two died when she dipped them in the freezing cold rivers. Her third child survived, and there are photos of her son that show his abnormal features. They dug up his skeleton after his death and found many characteristics very interesting in his skull and bone structure.

The snowman has been spotted from the Himalayas to Mount Everest. Many different expeditions have recovered evidence and had firsthand encounters with the elusive beast. A mummified hand, yeti skull, and hide were just some of the remnants that were discovered. The creatures crossed the great land bridge and spread to all the dense fortresses of the world.

Sadly, during the Vietnam War, soldiers had more to worry about than guns and bombs. A species of six-foot-tall hominids terrorized both sides of the army. Rock apes were originally given their name for their annoying habit of hitting soldiers with rocks. These creatures gave up positions, ruined camps and gave even the most hardened vet nightmares. The young men were told by their superiors to keep their mouths shut. In multiple occurrences, soldiers killed these creatures and couldn't believe their eyes.

In recent times, our troops have battled some creatures and partnered with others. In Afghanistan, an entire troop went offline. They sent in reinforcements and found all their equipment scattered, leading to a cave. They approached, and a giant spear was thrown in their direction. It sadly struck one of our soldiers, and he was killed. Out ran a giant red-haired man, and they opened fire. After hundreds of shots, the titan finally fell. They picked him up in a helicopter, and the verified incident is remembered as the Kandahar Giant. I have talked to a handful of soldiers who have been stationed over there, and they said that is just the story that got out to the public.

These creatures have surrounded us our entire lives. They roam the forests in our backyard and are on our children's TV screens. We have learned the way of the land from them, yet we still continue to take from their home. I believe the secret to our existence is much closer than most believe. Some ancient brothers reach out to us and the lucky ones of us listen. But sadly, people are still vanishing by the hundreds, so we need to be prepared with GPS locator beacons and firearms. But one day, I hope this world can have more friendships like Han and Chewie.

I hope you have enjoyed this adventure and learned a few things about the unknown creatures of our forest. Make sure to take all necessary safety precautions when entering the bush and prepare when planning an extended exhibition. Stay tuned to my SoundCloud and

Instagram for daily interviews and paranormal adventures. Tune into *Bigfoot Society, Sparks of the Paranormal, Induced Fear, Squatchcast, Science Meets Bigfoot, Rare and UNusual, Mysteries of Past & Present,* and *Our Different Take* if you want to hear me talk about my experiences with some experts in the field. Also check out Squatchin South Florida, Paranormal Highway, Standing Goats Rescue and anyone out there with boots on the ground! The stairs to the sky are worth the climb.

CHAPTER 19
LETTERS FROM FAMILY AND FRIENDS

Purcell

2001 summer... myself and one other... started from road to nowhere Bryson City up to clinicians Dome...

2nd night at campsite about 400 yards off trail... fire built... getting dark... about 35 to 50 yards away a large high pitched scream... followed by thrashing in the brush like both a fight and screaming... I've hiked 400 miles of Smokies... never heard an owl or bobcat scream like that... My friend and I were terrified... about an hour later a large tree pushed over across a trail 100 yards away... we broke camp... turned all our lamps on and broke camp... we crossed 4' tree at trail intersection... scared...

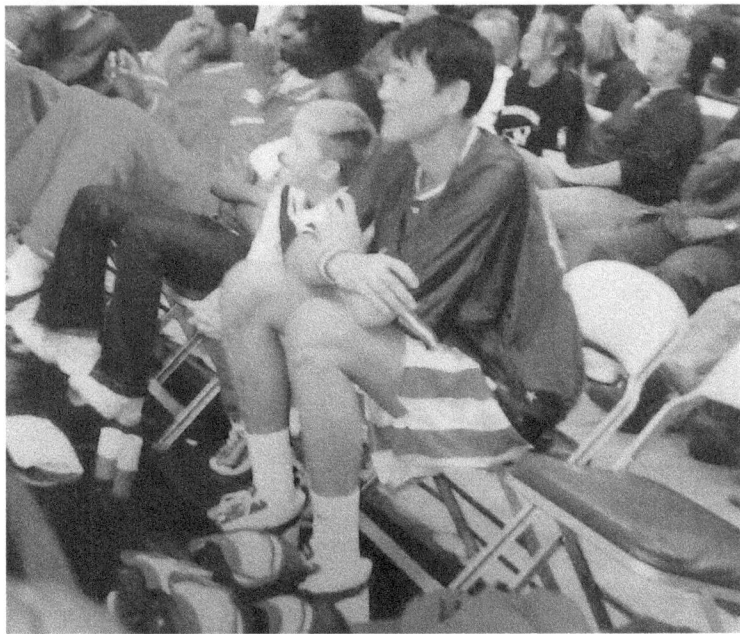

Giant genes? Harlem Globetrotter Giant, over seven feet tall

1982 on the coast of NC in coast guard... 82' CG drug boat, I was an officer of watch with one engineer witness... a bright light followed us for 3 hours... about 500 altitude about 2 miles behind... whatever course we took that night it followed... then blinked out around 3am...

Another giant, over seven foot tall college basketball player.

1999 in Troy, Ohio. Out on a clear night. Stars. About 10pm in October, looking at stars. Then the stars are gone and saw a large black triangle move over me, maybe 1000 feet. Slow. Silent. Then moved away and started back.

———

Neighbor

I'm sitting outside smoking. If you would have heard the noise I just heard, you'd flip tf out. It was a literal knock. Like someone beating a stick on a tree. Then like rustling in the distance.

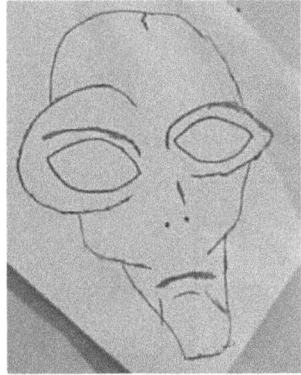

Sketch of the Lurker

———

Bryan

I had an encounter about six months ago near San Diego. I walked over to my car, and he must've been sitting behind my car watching us around the fire, and there was just two of us, and it literally stood up right in front of me, and it walked right by me. I could've touched it, and my friend ran over and lit it up with his iPhone, but it wasn't enough to fully see it. It froze in place and just stared us down. I

Native mound in Georgia

said hello friend twice but nothing. Once my friend turned the light off, it walked away...

Florida mound

———

Christy

This story is from 2018 June. What I saw was about six feet tall. The skin was a grayish green color. It blended in with the bark of the tree really well. The reason I was out there to begin with was to use the internet in my shed, and it was away from the noise in the house 'cause I was on TikTok at that time, and all the sudden my cat in the shed with me starts growling, and I heard swishing sounds of the grass, and I thought it was a deer, so I grabbed my flashlight, and I opened the door, and I looked, and I didn't see anything at first, and then all the sudden my light let me see its head peek around the tree, and it scared me when I saw it.

At first I just assumed it could have been neighbors because we were having trouble with the property, were seeing a lot of people at the time around the boundaries, like trying to scare us, because we bought the property, and apparently there was a bidding war at the time on the property, and we won. But after that I shined the light away because I was scared, and I shined it back cause I heard it rushing toward me really quick, and it was right there about 15 feet from me, and underneath his arms had a glow to it, like a blue translucent glow, and its eyes were giant round at the bottom but came to a point at the top.

Its eyes warped around its head in an upper diagonal slant. It had ridged eyebrows but no hair. There was no mouth, no nose, and it didn't even breathe 'cause when I had a light shined on it, it stayed still the whole time, and we just stared at each other. I held my breath, and it wasn't breathing either, and finally I decided I should run. Something told me just to run, so I put the flashlight behind me, and then I just took off for the house, and I got inside, and I was a nervous wreck, shaking, crying.

I woke my husband up, and I told him what happened, and I looked at the clock, and a whole hour had passed, and I knew we didn't stare at each other for an hour. So I don't know if I was abducted or if the time's wrong, but honestly I really think something is going on 'cause there's one hour of lost time there, and I know we didn't stare at each other for an hour, but my husband came out with his gun, and he went to where I saw it, and there was the track where it had gone around the tree, and it was going to come up and get me.

You could see right where it stopped. We looked around the property for a while, and we couldn't find it, and I almost called the police because I didn't know what to do, and so then I decided to just report it to MUFON, and an investigator contacted me back and asked me some questions, asked me if he could come on the property if I would let him, and I told him yeah, and there's been other reports around the area of sightings with an alien, so I don't know if he ever came out because he never called me to say he was coming to the property for sure.

He never posted the picture I got that I used for the video that was never posted to MUFON with my report. They have a habit of not posting the pictures with the report if it's a really good picture, but they sent me forms and asked me to draw it, and I drew it for them, and it was very muscular where the shoulder area is, like it was tall and muscular at the top part, but then it got slender in the hip area.

After that sighting I got very scared to be outside, and I loved being outside at night. I was always having bonfires and staying up super late just to have a fire outside at night, but after that you wouldn't see me outside at night even as the sun was setting for over a year. It got to where I didn't even want to be outside during the day on that property because stuff started happening during the day.

I would see orbs floating around over the field, I saw a lady with some kind of scarf shroud walking across my field, but she was transparent, and my daughter saw this black elf creature just appear out of nowhere and then like run with super hyper speed and disappear, and it was wearing like this weird hat that was pointed, and she never saw anything else like that again. That was right before we moved 'cause when they started having experiences with my kids, we decided enough's enough, we need to just get off this property.

So we found another place to rent out and live, and we still own the property, so we're keeping up with the payments for that just so I can go investigate. My son, he would see something white in the field, and he would describe it as being really tall hunched over and furry, and at the time I didn't know, but there's been a lot of bigfoot sightings around the area that have white fur, and that's over in Allegheny County at Black Creek area and Belfast.

I am in New York. They would hear a tapping on the window and would hear knocking on the door. My dogs would hear stuff. My husband works a lot, long hours, so he wasn't home for a lot of it. One night I was outside by the car, and all the sudden I just heard this really loud growl, and it echoed in my chest like fireworks booming, and it sounded like a grizzly. There was nothing in front of me, and it was invisible, whatever it was. So I jumped in my car, and I started wailing on the horn. After I calmed down, I went inside.

The Kolomoki Pyramid

I've had stuff happen to me since I was a kid. We used to live in this old farmhouse, and I would see things in the house. We would hear footsteps in the house. It used to be a funeral parlor. When I was younger, about three years old, the bed would levitate up off the floor. Cabinets would slam open and shut. We would hear people pull into the driveway, and we look out and no one would be there, and I would constantly have my mom hold me because I was so scared. I would see some lady and tell my mom to make her stop looking at me.

I do remember seeing a lot of ghosts when I was younger. There was a man, he would wear flannel and stand out the window holding an axe, and he had red eyes, and he would signal his finger for me to come here, and I would just tell my mom, and it got to the point to where my mom did start believing because the cabinets would slam shut, and she would actually yell at them to stop it.

Eventually we moved out because of what was going on, but stuff has always followed my family. We have a history of psychics in our family, so we're definitely sensitive to that kind of stuff and probably why it follows us around.

———

Alexander

I barely moved to the city of Beaumont in the county of Rivuyerside, CA. I worked at a job called Green Thumb in the city of Banning, CA. These cities are side by side. Anyway I was invited to a house party by a coworker in Banning.

Sketch of Crawler

My coworker couldn't drive me back home because he was very drunk. I had no car at the time. I just started this job, about 3 weeks in. I REALLY didn't know anyone personally.

So I decided to walk home. Someone from the party gave me vague directions to Beaumont, so I started to walk. I'm walking for about 3 hours nonstop on a road called Ramsey Ave. I pass my job, I see the warehouse Green Thumb, to the north side heading West on Ramey is nothing but dirt fields, after the fields are mountains.

At this point walking for 3 hours, I'm very alert, sober and driven to get home, I look to my right, and I see this humanoid "thing" sitting on its butt, with its legs crossed. The face was peach in color with dark hair around its entire face except its mouth, nose, eyes and forehead.

I stopped. I sort of walked past it as I was assessing what this could be. This is literally in the middle of NOWHERE.

Sketch of Ohio Grassman

I stopped, I took just a few steps towards it, and my instincts IMMEDIATELY hit me that this was a living thing. My brain controlled my body and drove me back step the heck back when I saw its entire figure. This thing was REAL, expressionless, sitting with its legs crossed on the dirt field. It was VERY dark. The only light was the road light posts.

I immediately started to walk away from it. I was very, very afraid. For the next couple of hours of walking home, I kept looking back constantly. This really happened. I will go on any record and say it the same. It WILL NEVER CHANGE. This was in 2017 in Banning, CA.

———

CW

My dad, my neighbor, and I were at Look and Tremble. We like to swim, throw sticks, and ride real fast on the gravel roads. It's pretty far back in the woods and along the Chipola River. Many kayaks, canoes and tubes go over the rapids. My 5th grade teacher did a video on Look and Tremble on Two Egg TV on YouTube. There is a history of poisonous snakes, religious handlers and buried treasure. We go out there on Halloween and eclipses. But our encounter happened on just an ordinary day.

It was late evening. I was digging in the sand with a stick while my dad took a smoke. After a while I took a log and banged it on the nearby tree. I was trying to spook my dad but was also calling bigfoot. My first hit was bad, my grip was loose, and it hurt my hands. The guys looked at me and waited for me to do it right. I muscled up and wound up and took a big hit like an ax, and all of a sudden I heard a tree crash down really loud across the river. We all halted in our steps and listened closely. The surrounding forest was still and silent. We sensed something was watching us, and we were right out in the open. My neighbor was scared something was gonna take me from the water. My dad was just ready to go. But honestly I wanted more because I was interested.

In the Void

If it wanted to hurt us, I think it would already have gotten us. I think it was just curious and saw me playing. We cruised out of there, and I watched outside our back window just to see if anything was following us. Luckily we made it home alive. Every time I'm back there, I think of that evening.

———

Tony & Adriana

The night had begun to set at 6 p.m. when Tony was driving home with his sister. The final curve before they were to hit the dirt road to take them, Tony had spotted what looked like a dead rattlesnake illuminated by the headlights on the right side of the road.

Tony told his sister to stop while he opened the door and took a step outside of the car. A foot away from the snake, he sensed a presence nearby. Looking up, there stood a three foot dog staring at him, barely noticeable from the shadows.

Strange animal track

The dog had patches of fur sticking out like it had intense mange. With its skeletal-like body and twisted jaw and crooked fangs gripping the head of the snake, it continued to stare at Tony until he jumped back into the car and yelled at his sister to drive. They sped onto the dirt road until the creature in the background was out of sight.

Loren Coleman and me at Great Florida Bigfoot Conference

Adriana was used to traveling, so it wasn't unusual for her and her family to be in a motel. This was when she was about 6 years old. She was sitting quietly on one of the double beds closest to the wall while her parents were watching the news on the foot of their bed, which was next to the closet. Bored, she looked at her surroundings when she noticed a man hiding in the closet. He looked to be in his fifties, wearing a white T-shirt and jeans.

She stared at this man, who was staring at her parents like they were the scariest thing that he had ever seen. He was cowering behind the closet door, standing perfectly still when he then looked at Adriana. He froze as they made eye contact as they stared at each other for a full minute. He then swiftly turned around and ran back into the closet. Curious, she got off of her bed and walked to the closet. She looked inside it and checked the sides.

The man was gone, so she shrugged it off and went to sit back on her bed. It wasn't until it was time to go to sleep that she thought about the man again and came to the realization that what she had seen was a ghost. Did that ghost realize that he was dead and he was scared, or did he not know? What Adriana can remember the most is the look of raw fear that his expression held was something that she would never see again.

Michelle

I began my mediumship journey at age three. I had a very sheltered childhood, therefore I had no idea what a "monster" was. I was very limited on things I was allowed to watch on television and, also, what was spoken within my vicinity. Bedtime was a tormenting thought because every night I encountered the spirit realm. I would be awakened by hearing footsteps and heavy breathing beside my bed. I would hear my parents snoring in their bedroom, and there was no other living person in our home. I remember going to sleep each night with my blanket over my head, leaving just the tip of my nose peeking out in order to get fresh air. I slept with a stuffed dog that we named Old Henry. He helped me feel safe only briefly during these encounters. I would become frozen in bed. I dared not to visibly breathe. I believed if I didn't move that whatever was beside my bed would leave. I would breathe slow and shallow until I could feel and hear the entity leaning over my body. I then would scream in horror, "Mommy!"

My mother would rush in to comfort me, explaining that it was only a bad dream. Eventually my mother would fall asleep while holding me in her loving arms. At one point, I began being choked while in bed, but completely awake. My bedroom doors would slam open and shut repetitively. My mother put an open Bible inside my closet, and it slowed down the activity. I would also sleep hugged up to a Bible for many years to come. Night after night this continued throughout my childhood. As I had gotten older, I began to visibly see spirits. Many times they felt very negative, and I could feel them staring at me throughout the day, especially in the hallways, no matter where I lived. I had recurring dreams of being chased by a demonic shadow for years.

From the movie, The Void Cat

As an older child, it became the normal household talk that our home was haunted. Again, no matter where we lived. As I had grown into adulthood and moved away from my parents to begin my own journey in life, I began to notice that everywhere I lived had the same result. I couldn't sleep at night due to pure terror. I was a grown woman and had to sleep with every light on, while continuing to fight sleep. It was extremely hard to function during the day, resulting in working evening and night shifts so that I could get some sleep during the day. However, this didn't always work. I would wake up to hearing my name being called, a gentle tug of my hair, or hear people talking that I didn't physically see. During this time, I began having visions while awake and asleep. I would see things that would become true.

Bootleggers treasure

When in my early forties, in 2015, I became very ill. I had a very rare accident several years prior and, some time after, had a product placed in my body in hopes of returning to as "normal" as possible. I did well for many years until my body rejected the product. Soon after, I had many back-to-back surgeries, and my body was not healing as it should have. I eventually had become bedridden, and the pain I endured was too intense. I felt as if I was dying. I then screamed out to God, saying, "Yahweh, if I'm going to die, show me the truth!" My thoughts in that moment were that there were so many beliefs, all claiming to be "the right" faith, that I wanted to make sure I was practicing correctly in order to make it to heaven.

Immediately as I screamed out, I felt a man's hand gently pat my mid-back twice. I heard this man say, "I'll be right back." The voice was familiar to someone who was in my life and passed during my childhood. I turned my head but saw no one. I then saw a female extraterrestrial as I turned my head forward. She was more beautiful than any female could possibly be on Earth without extensive surgery. She had large pouty lips, large perfectly shaped breasts and buttocks. She was extremely thin and approximately 7 ½ feet tall. She was standing at attention with her elbows bent and hands behind her back. She had no apparent hair.

The most amazing thing was, she was wearing some sort of remarkably thin off-white material. I could see every outline and crevice of her lips and body, including her eyeballs and lashes. She appeared to be African American. I gazed in awe at this female. She was wearing boots up to her calves. What I found very odd was this suit had no zippers, buttons, nor Velcro that I could see. I couldn't understand how she applied her suit over her entire body, but without open areas to do so. I felt only love and tranquility. This extraterrestrial female spoke telepathically, stating these words softly, "Everything is ok. All is well." Suddenly, she disappeared into a silver, shiny, glittery type of dust.

All of a sudden, I was up within the galaxy. I was within, and enveloped within, the love of God! I felt nothing but complete and total love. I then realized that God was, is, and always will be LOVE. I had no thought of Earth, nor my family and friends; not even my husband nor children, who are everything to me in this life. I was given a knowing that my creator is not a certain religion, nor do we ever die! Only our physical bodies pass, and our spirits continue without end.

Not so ancient ruins…at a Putt Putt course in Ohio

I was no longer afraid to die. In addition, I was given a message to release all fear. As this event was taking place, I saw the female extraterrestrial that had been inside my bedroom appear as a clear giant. She was the size of the sun magnified approximately fifteen times. She appeared with only a hint of white so that I could see her. She was some sort of energy with the appearance of clear plasma. The stars outlined this female body and hair. Her hair appeared the length of her body, swaying, as she was dancing somewhat like a ballerina. I felt her peace and happiness. Then, as fast as I had been taken into the galaxy, I met my physical body with a hard re-entrance, shaking the entire bed and waking my husband. This is when my life truly began!

Since this out-of-body experience, all psychic abilities that I am aware of opened up drastically. I travel through portals, wake up on spacecraft (usually lying on a table), have met many different races of benevolent extraterrestrial beings that look anywhere from human to what I call "Bird" people (half human, half bird). I have encountered a reptilian snake-like being that took away my pain, a malevolent octopus being. I travel (astral travel and remote view) and am currently learning to control this. I see, hear, feel, smell, taste the spirit realms. While awake I have many visions that I call "video clip visions" that come true. Many times throughout my days I see triangles and pyramids floating in 3D when I blink. I also see geometry equations in 3D as well. I communicate with angels, spirit guides, Jesus, the ascended masters, those who have passed into spirit form. Again, I was not this open to the spirit realms until the out-of-body event.

One of my most interesting extraterrestrial encounters occurred while I was still mostly bedfast. This event happened approx. 2016. I was awakened as I usually am at 3:00 a.m. give or take a few minutes. This time, it was a new being. YES, bigfoot was standing at the foot of my bed! He was a holograph and stood approximately 8 feet tall, due to our ceiling height, and his head was flush with the ceiling. He spoke to me telepathically, explaining the following: What humans call bigfoot are an extraterrestrial race. This is why it is hard to find actual physical evidence in the form of a body. They have the ability to move from their realm into ours quickly, and vice versa.

It was also explained that the reason this extraterrestrial race is known to throw rocks and growl at humans when encountered in the woods, is due to they can become ill if they come into close contact with humans, as humans can become ill by being too close to their E.T. race. They come here to help watch over the Earth, helping to maintain energy for plant life and the energy of animals. They don't want to harm us, but be assured if a bigfoot species is confronted, it will take all means necessary to scare the human away. It is for our protection, and theirs.

I now have learned to let go of the fear I was asked to release a few years ago. I am walking and feel very blessed. I "came out" publicly regarding these abilities a few months ago after years of ridicule. I decided to be strong for others who are afraid of speaking of their paranormal experiences due to humiliation. I also have started telling of my personal experiences on several social media platforms to help those who have children feeling tormented by the spirit realms. I don't have all the answers, but I will continue searching for explanations. Many blessings, Michelle Brandenburg-Rogers, The Paranormal Experiencer

————

Brittany

I was sitting on the stoop of my back door, smoking a cigarette like the badass 15 year old I thought I was. My mom was already in bed, and my father was at work. It was 12-1am I would say. I had lit the tiki torches nearby to keep the devilish mosquitoes at bay. I started hearing footsteps approaching in the dry leaves. I tried to rationalize it, but there was no wind, and all the animals were inside for the night. I got the courage to ask if someone was there. I received no response. All sounds had ceased. I asked again. No response, just silence. I had my wits about me enough to ask for a sign of their presence. Again nothing.

I then said, "If there is someone here with me, blow out the torch." A few seconds later the flame on the tiki went flat as if someone had tried to blow it out. At that moment I flicked my cigarette into the yard, blew out the torch and ran inside. 3 months later I had finally

CONNOR FLYNN

convinced my mom to leave my alcoholic father, and we
moved out. I never returned to that house.

The Green Clawed Beast of the Ohio River

I was 17 years old when I had my last experience. I
was at my boyfriend's house. We were sitting out front
talking when I noticed the old lady across the street turn
on her light and peer through her window. This was a
pretty normal occurrence. Anytime we were outside, she
would do this. It's been a few weeks since I'd been over
to his house. I'd been out of town for the holidays. My
boyfriend didn't react like it was normal and wanted to
go inside.

172

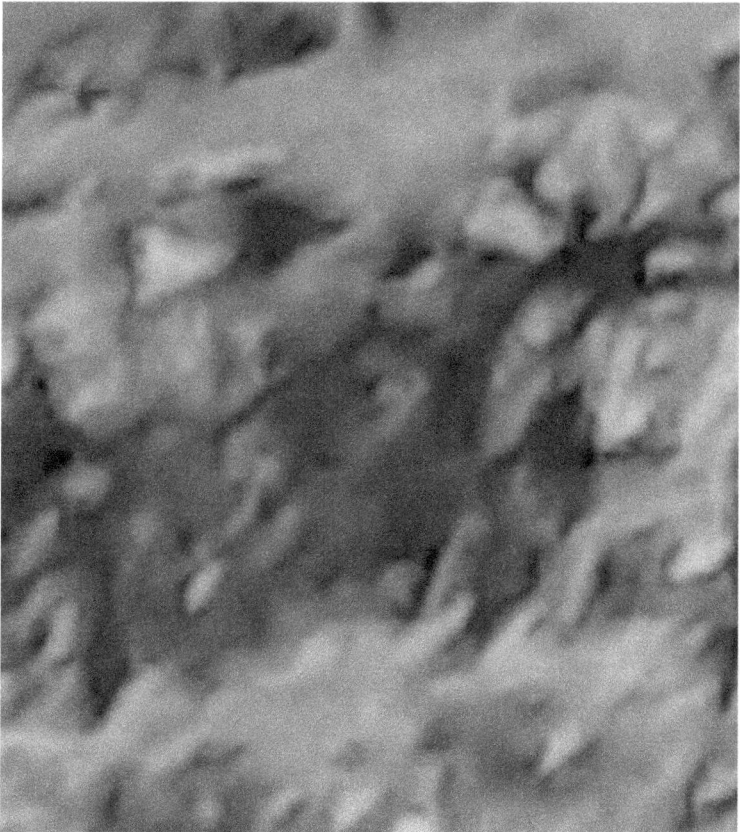

My Florida Skunk Ape photo. In center you can make out a
dark face, eyeball, and prominent cheek bone.

When I asked him why, he told me the ambulance
had come a week ago and taken the old lady out of the
house on a stretcher. The neighbor had said she had a
heart attack and died that night. No family had come to
collect her belongings or anything. Her car was still
parked in the driveway, and her trashcan was still on the
curb. I have no doubt we had seen her ghost.

———

Baker

To further elaborate on what I saw as a kid and the experiences that followed. My house I grew up in as a child, we had a couch in the living room right under a big window that looked out across the street to the neighbor's yard where there were some power lines at. Well, in the middle power line I saw three glowing orbs almost like three little suns just slightly different in its composition without the burning intensity on the eyes while looking at them. I did feel a type of warmth at that time I yet can't explain to this day. Looking at them though, when I saw them, I told my grandma and mom, as I was freaking out, so when they both came to look through the window at the same time as I, they couldn't see them, but I still could.

At the time I was raised on Catholic beliefs from my grandma, so I assumed they were angels and told Grandma they were past relatives of ours on her side of the family checkin' in on us, but today thinking back, I dunno what they were or what they were up to, but what I saw and felt back then as I saw them… and am unsure of them still, but it instilled a belief in me that's as strong as ever today that there is more to life than what meets the eye. After that, the following months I had these visions like dreams, dreams of stages in my life sort of like chapters in a book.

Sketch of the Goblin

They were vivid enough to where when I'd reach these moments in life, I'd have a deja vu moment like I experienced/lived it before but vague enough to where I couldn't tell when the next chapter would occur. Everything I've dreamed from that time period has come true... And they're still happening, haven't had one of those moments in a while, but I feel like another one's coming up soonish. The visions in particular weren't of any sort of importance other than the personal meaning behind them, that I am right where I'm supposed to be in life even through all the tears from the hardships I've faced.

Hiram Worden carving in Hinckley, Ohio

Along came a spider, crawling down the web, bit the insect with a bit of poison. But what it didn't know is the insect's blood was twice as venomous as the spider's poison. Was a setup from the start, another way of art, being close to death, still coming out on top. Took a bit of time and a good amount of pain, the insect found a bug that was killed by the eight. The insect took it back and opened up its chest. And took a few samples of the spider's venom. Once... every day, it battled the pain, injecting itself, increasing each day. Built a tolerance, but the poison was so strong, it needed something between, like shielded by a shell. So it went on the hunt and found another bug. Twice its size but still took it down. With the shell and some heart, it headed to the web. The spider attacked, but he was ready for that. The spider went down and broke its own web. The bug climbed through, found his wife and kids!

ABOUT THE AUTHOR

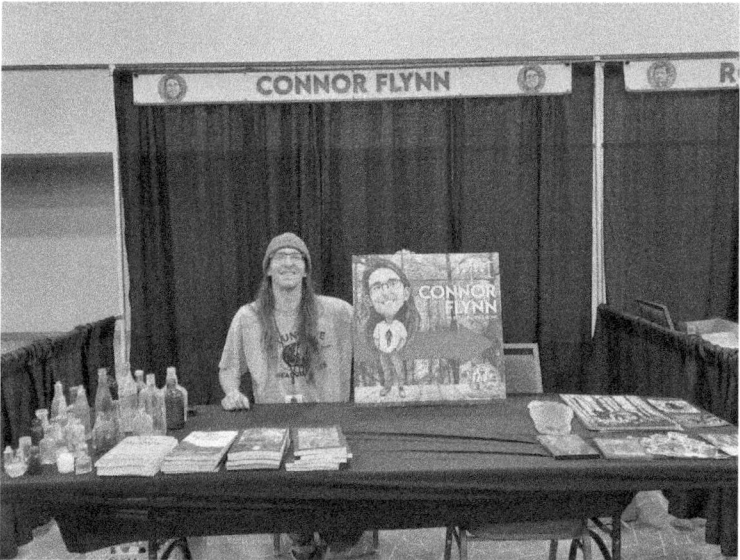

Connor Flynn is originally from the coast of Lake Erie and now resides in the Florida Panhandle. His love for outdoors and investigative journalism has led him down many paths of strange and unusual things. Flynn has appeared in films "Zillafoot" and "The Void Cat" and hosts a horror themed podcast. Catch Connor in the swamp or on the screen, he stays active in the field always waiting for a scream!

Visit him at his YouTube Channel below and on other social media platforms.

YouTube: https://www.youtube.com/channel/UCvcN_fkxz1wtjgwibEtF6qQ

ALSO BY CONNOR FLYNN

Erie Swamps: Road Trip to Eden

www.ingramcontent.com/pod-product-compliance
Lightning Source LLC
Chambersburg PA
CBHW030013290326
41934CB00005B/317